Crossroads Café

TEACHER'S RESOURCE BOOK B

Crossroads Café
TEACHER'S RESOURCE BOOK B

Elizabeth Minicz

HEINLE & HEINLE PUBLISHERS

I(T)P *An International Thomson Publishing Company*

Boston, Massachusetts 02116 U.S.A.

New York • London • Bonn • Boston • Detroit • Madrid • Melbourne • Mexico City • Paris •
Singapore • Tokyo • Toronto • Washington • Albany, NY • Belmont, CA • Cincinnati, OH

The publication of *Crossroads Café* was directed by the members of the Heinle & Heinle Secondary and Adult ESL Publishing Team.

Senior Editorial Director:	Roseanne Mendoza
Senior Production Services Coordinator:	Lisa McLaughlin
Market Development Director:	Jonathan Boggs

Also participating in the publication of the program were:

Vice President and Publisher, ESL:	Stanley Galek
Developmental Editor:	Sally Conover
Production Editor:	Maryellen Killeen
Manufacturing Coordinator:	Mary Beth Hennebury
Full Service Design and Production:	PC&F, Inc.

ISBN: 0-8384-64343

Heinle & Heinle is a division of International Thomson Publishing, Inc.

TABLE OF CONTENTS

ACKNOWLEDGMENTS

With heartfelt thanks to the entire Crossroads Café team and especially Roseanne Mendoza, whose invitation to join the team delighted and challenged me; Sally Conover, whose expert editorial skills, ceaseless enthusiasm, constant encouragement, and infinite patience enabled me to complete an awesome task; and Lynn Savage, whose amazing abilities continue to inspire me.

CROSSROADS CAFÉ—SUMMARIES OF UNITS 1 TO 13

1 Opening Day

Victor Brashov is ready to open a new restaurant, but the restaurant doesn't have a name or workers.

2 Growing Pains

Henry has problems with working at the café. A health and safety inspector visits the café.

3 Worlds Apart

Rosa's boyfriend arrives from Mexico, and she must make a difficult decision. Mr. Brashov has trouble sleeping.

4 Who's the Boss?

Jamal sees two old friends. They think he's the owner of the café.

5 Lost and Found

Katherine's son has behavior problems in school. He gets help from someone. Jess and Carol's house is robbed.

6 Time is Money

An efficiency expert comes to look at the café. Rosa has problems with her night school class.

7 Fish Out of Water

Mr. Brashov's brother arrives from Romania. He finds that life in the United States is different from life in his country.

8 Family Matters

Katherine takes a second job to make more money. Rosa teaches Henry to dance.

9 Rush to Judgment

Jamal is a suspect in a robbery. Henry's grandparents get lost in the city.

10 Let the Buyer Beware

Mr. Brashov meets a woman who promises to improve the café's business. He goes out on several dates with her. Katherine also goes out on a date.

11 No Vacancy

Rosa wants to move into a new apartment, but she has problems. Henry works on a journalism project.

12 Turning Points

Someone breaks into the café. Rosa learns to drive.

13 Trading Places

The café employees change jobs for a day. Jess and Carol have problems at home.

INTRODUCTION

This **Teacher's Resource Book** will help you use the *Crossroads Café* program effectively. Designed as a planning guide for teachers, it provides a wealth of communicative activities that enhance learner interaction with *Crossroads Café* materials. It can be used by both classroom teachers and tutors who work with large groups. The separate **Partner Guide** is designed for tutors who provide one-to-one or small group instruction.

The **Teacher's Resource Book** includes:

♦ A comprehensive introduction to the *Crossroads Café* program
♦ Specific ideas and instructions for the 13 episodes of the worktext, including four reproducible handouts per episode
♦ A glossary of teaching techniques and terminology
♦ A checklist for learners to use to reflect on learning

The twenty questions and answers that follow explain how to use the components of the **Teacher's Resource Book** with the *Crossroads Café* materials.

1. HOW DO I USE THE WORKTEXT?

The *Crossroads Café* worktext is designed for independent learners; therefore, it provides answer keys for almost all exercises. One way to integrate the independent activities in the worktext with classroom activities is to get feedback from learners on activities they do outside of class. For suggestions, see the section on **Class Openers** on page xii, Question #10.

Several activities in the worktext are open-ended exercises with no "right" or "wrong" answers and therefore lend themselves to follow-up in the classroom. They are:

1. The activity in **In Your Community** that encourages learners to collect and compare actual life skills reading documents to the examples in the worktext
2. The writing portion of **Read and Write**
3. The discussion element in **What Do You Think?**

Finally, the extension activities and handouts contained in the Notes section for specific units relate back to sections of the worktext. Prior to beginning each of these activities, teachers may want to discuss how the activities relate to the worktext.

2. WHO SHOULD USE THE PHOTO STORIES?

The primary purpose of the **Photo Stories** is to provide a previewing activity for viewers with low-level English proficiency. The **Photo Stories** will:

♦ Assist learners in following the main story line when they view the video
♦ Provide learners with high-success, low-stress follow-up activities
♦ Help learners at higher levels preview and review the story line

The frames in the **Photo Stories** follow the main plot of the story and do not include the **Culture Clips** or **Word Plays**.

3. HOW CAN THE PHOTO STORIES BE USED?

Here are some general ideas for ways to use each of the **Photo Stories**.

♦ Have learners explain what happened in between the frames in the **Photo Stories**. This is best done with parts of the story rather than the whole story.

- Have learners look at a group of frames and have them discuss what else happens in the video that isn't shown in the frames.
- Select a scene of six to eight frames. Cover (or white out) the speech bubbles and give learners photocopies of those pages. Have learners write what the characters are saying.
- Have learners tell the whole story or pieces of the story in their own words.
- Have learners role-play situations depicted in the frames.
- Have learners compare and contrast characters in a specific episode using *Venn Diagrams*.
- Have learners write the vocabulary words from **Build Your Vocabulary** on small cards and categorize them according to parts of speech, word families, opposites, synonyms, and so on.
- Encourage learners to add other new words to the **Picture Dictionary**.
- Have learners create sentences, orally or written, using the words in the **Picture Dictionary**.
- Have learners write questions about the words in the **Picture Dictionary**.

4. HOW SHOULD I STRUCTURE THE CLASS TIME?

Schools will set up the *Crossroads Café* distance learning program in a variety of ways. Depending on the amount of time spent with learners, teachers will adjust their plans and activities.

- If there is only one class meeting for each episode, then see the suggestions for episode openers (on page xi, in Question #6) and **Episode Wrap-Up** on pages xii–xiii, Question #12. Each class begins with activities to "wrap up" the episode learners watched before class and ends with activities to prepare learners for the episode they will watch before the next class.
- If there is more than one class meeting for each episode, you may want to group learning activities as described below.

   If there are two class sessions per episode, each class session could focus on two sets of activities identified in the chart **Teacher's Notes at a Glance** (for example, **Your New Language** and **In Your Community** in session 1 and **What Do You Think?** and **Culture Clip** in session 2).

- If your time with learners is limited, select the activities on the *reproducible handouts* and skip the *extension activities*.

5. HOW CAN I MONITOR LEARNERS' INDEPENDENT WORK?

One way to monitor learners' independent work is to have learners keep a journal.

- Encourage all levels of learners to write in a journal every day—at home and in class.
- Have learners start by writing for only five minutes.
- Tell learners to write vocabulary words or characters' names from *Crossroads Café* if they can't think of words to write. In a short time, learners will be surprised at how much they have to say.
- Read and respond to learners' journal entries as often as possible. If you have a large class, you might want to collect, read, and comment on only five or six journals at a time.

Another way to monitor learners' independent work is to review completed exercises and checklists in the worktext.

6. HOW DO I BEGIN AN EPISODE?

An episode opener prepares learners to view an episode for the first time by stimulating their prior knowledge. Here are some suggestions for episode openers.

- Call learners' attention to the title in either the Photo Stories or Worktext. Discuss what they think it means.
- Ask learners to look at the opening photo and describe what they see in either the Photo Stories or Worktext. Ask these questions or make up your own.

   Who do you see?
   Where are the people?
   What are they doing?
   What are they saying?
   What are they thinking?
   How do they feel?
   Have you ever done this?
   Have you ever felt like this?
   Why is this episode called _____?

- Ask learners to read the summary and share answers to the question below the opening photo in the Photo Stories.
- Look at the photos and read the text in the Photo Stories.
- Have learners complete the **Before You Watch** exercises in the worktext.
- Have learners read questions in the **Focus for Watching** section of the worktext.

7. HOW DO I USE THE *TEACHER'S NOTES AT A GLANCE* AND *VIDEO HIGHLIGHTS* CHARTS THAT BEGIN EACH UNIT?

The **Teacher's Notes at a Glance** chart provides a quick overview of activities, materials, and suggested times for activities contained in the notes for each unit. The chart does the following:

- helps you choose which activities in the **Teacher's Resource Book** you want learners to do. If the chart mentions an activity with which you are unfamiliar, such as *3-step interview*, you can check the **Glossary** for an explanation. (All the italicized terms are found in the Glossary.)
- shows where to find supplementary, interactive activities for specific sections of the learner worktext
- tells what materials are needed for each activity—TV/VCR, blackboard, paper, scissors, and so on
- gives a general idea of how much time to spend on each activity

The *Video Highlights* chart:

- identifies the content of the **Word Play** and **Culture Clip** segments of the video episode
- highlights the **Story Clips** that are mentioned in the first chart and used in the general notes which follow
- provides time code references to help you locate video clips

> **Note:** *The time codes on the chart are found on the closed caption setting #2. Any TV manufactured after July 1993 is equipped with a closed-caption decoder. If your TV does not have the closed caption capacity, you might want to note the counter times on your machine and write them in the chart for future reference. If you have an earlier model TV, decoder boxes providing access to the closed caption channel can be purchased. For more information on closed captioning, you can call the Closed Captioning Institute at 1-800-533-WORD.*

8. WHAT FOLLOWS THE CHARTS IN EACH UNIT?

The charts are followed by several pages which elaborate on the activities and video clips listed in the charts. Descriptions and instructions are provided for the reproducible handouts and the extension activities. The video clips mentioned in the chart are described and ideas for showing and working with the clips are presented.

> **Note:** *If a section of the worktext is not listed in the chart, it simply means no expansion activities have been identified. It does not mean that learners should skip the worktext pages.*

9. WHAT KINDS OF ACTIVITIES ARE FOUND IN THE TEACHER'S NOTES?

Because the majority of the activities in the worktext are designed for independent use, the **Teacher's Resource Books** contain suggestions for interactive and collaborative activities to be done in groups. With this goal in mind, learners should spend the majority of class or tutoring time practicing oral language.

- The activities typically begin with a whole class discussion followed by pair or small group work.
- The partner and group work provide learners with opportunities to practice English and to apply what they've learned from the video, the worktexts, and from each other.
- *Cooperative learning structures* are frequently used in the activities because they promote practice and participation. All of the *cooperative learning structures* mentioned in the notes, such as *corners, think-pair-share* and *roundrobin* are explained in the **Glossary.**

10. HOW CAN I BEGIN EACH CLASS MEETING?

Every unit begins with a **Class Opener.** What you do for a **Class Opener** will vary according to what learners did the last time you met with them. Refer back to this page for ideas for **Class Openers** or make up your own.

- Talk about what learners have been doing, (for example, watching videos, doing homework) since you last met with them.
- Review or summarize video episodes learners have seen on their own.
- Review previously completed worktext pages or review and share any homework assignments.
- Find out which areas learners want to concentrate on during this class meeting.
- Have learners reflect on which activities were most or least helpful, most or least enjoyable.
- Have learners discuss watching the videos. Ask how many times they watched, how they watched (in one sitting, with interruptions, over several days, and so on), and with whom they watched.
- Ask learners to take turns retelling the story to a partner, in a small group, or to the class. Or have students write the story.

11. WHAT ARE THE STORY CLIPS AND HOW DO I USE THEM?

There are two-to-four **Story Clips** in each unit.

Story Clips are video scenes selected to replay in class. They highlight the language focus and provide active listening practice or provide additional opportunities for discussion and writing. Sometimes they focus attention on the main plot of the episode; other times they involve the subplot. The video techniques used with the clips such as *prediction, freeze frame,* and *behavior study* are explained in the **Glossary.**

The **Video Highlights** charts contain a brief summary of the scene and the time code. This will help you locate a scene when you replay it for learners.

12. WHAT IS AN EPISODE WRAP-UP?

An **Episode Wrap-Up** is the final activity learners do in a unit before they **Check Their English** and move on to the next episode. The **Episode Wrap-Up** provides closure. To conclude an episode, do one or more of the following.

♦ Discuss the meaning of the title.
♦ Have learners write about the meaning of the title.
♦ Have learners retell or rewrite the story in their own words.
♦ Ask learners to predict what will happen next to the characters.
♦ Personalize the story. Ask learners to discuss or write about similar events in their lives.
♦ Have learners discuss or write about the characters. Ask if they have ever met anyone like a particular character in the episode.
♦ Have learners write in a journal about some aspect of the video, for example, the topic, characters, or situations.

13. WHAT IS THE PURPOSE OF THE REPRODUCIBLE HANDOUTS?

The **Handouts** link interaction activities to specific sections of the worktext. The chart below shows where the handouts are found in most episodes. However, there may be two **Handouts** for one worktext section when the language focus or the content is particularly challenging.

WORKTEXT SECTION	HANDOUT
YOUR NEW LANGUAGE	HANDOUT A
IN YOUR COMMUNITY	HANDOUT B
WHAT DO YOU THINK?	HANDOUT C
CULTURE CLIP	HANDOUT D

14. HOW DO I USE THE REPRODUCIBLE HANDOUTS?

The guidelines below help you to:

♦ prepare the handouts for learners
♦ ensure learners success in using the handouts
♦ provide follow-up activities

Here are some ideas for preparing the handouts.

- ◆ If possible, photocopy the handouts on card stock; they will be more durable and will last longer. If you store them in labeled envelopes, they can be used again and again.
- ◆ Use the handouts after learners have completed worktext pages or watched the video. They should not be used to introduce or present new language—grammar and/or vocabulary. Learners will not be able to do the handouts successfully if the language and concepts are new to them.
- ◆ Although some handouts tell learners to work in a small or in a large group, the handouts may be used by two learners working as a pair.
- ◆ Handouts that need to be cut have dotted lines with a scissors icon. Whenever possible, have learners themselves cut and scramble the strips or cards used in the handouts. This will decrease your preparation time.

Here are some ideas for ensuring learner success.

- ◆ Explain the purpose of the handouts to learners. Stress that the handouts provide additional opportunities to practice the language and vocabulary of the videos and worktext, to exchange information and ideas with other learners.
- ◆ Model the activities so learners have a clear understanding of how to work with a partner or in a group.
- ◆ Review the directions orally. Ask learners if they have any questions.
- ◆ Monitor learners while they do the activities.
- ◆ Provide follow-up.

Here are some ideas for follow-up.

- ◆ Use cooperative learning structures such as *stand-up-and-share, best idea only,* and *teams share* to provide feedback. See the **Glossary** for definitions and examples.
- ◆ Post learners' work, when appropriate, on the walls for learners to read.
- ◆ Have pairs or small groups share role-plays with the rest of the class.
- ◆ Have learners reflect on their participation by asking themselves questions such as:

    "How well did I understand the activity?"
    "How much did I participate?"
    "Was I a good listener?"

- ◆ Have learners write about the activities in their journals.

15. WHAT IS THE PURPOSE OF THE ONE-PAGE SUMMARIES AT THE END OF EACH UNIT?

There are two main purposes for the **Summaries**:

- ◆ to provide teachers and tutors with a summary of the video episode
- ◆ to provide a resource for additional activities for learners

    Note: *The **Summaries** are written at a high-beginning/low-intermediate learner level.*

    To see if the reading level of the summaries is appropriate for learners in your class, cover every seventh word and follow the directions in Option #4 on the next page. If learners identify less than 40% of the words correctly, don't use the summaries—they are too difficult.

16. HOW DO I USE THE SUMMARIES WITH LEARNERS?

Below are some options for using the summaries.

Option #1

- Make a photocopy of the summary for each learner.
- Have learners read it silently, as quickly as possible.
- Ask learners *yes/no, either/or,* and *wh- questions* about the content.
- Have learners read it again silently.

Option #2

- Have learners follow along while you read the summary aloud.
- As you read, change words (use synonyms or antonyms) and have learners correct you.

Option #3

- Make additional photocopies of the summary.
- Cut each copy into separate strips (one set for each learner or pair of learners).
- Scramble the strips and have learners put them in the correct order.

Option #4

- Retype the summary and delete selected words or cover selected words before you photocopy it. Make sure you leave the first and last lines intact.
- Have learners fill in the missing words.

Option #5

- Retype the summary and delete words, but don't leave spaces where the words were.
- Have learners read silently or follow along while you read aloud.
- Instruct learners to put a caret (^) every place a word is missing.

17. WHAT'S IN THE GLOSSARY?

The **Glossary** contains explanations and examples of *cooperative learning structures, video techniques,* and other technical terms used in the **Teacher's Resource Book.**

18. HOW DO LEARNERS RECORD PROGRESS?

Successful language learners take responsibility for their learning in a variety of ways. They select appropriate learning strategies to assist them in planning, monitoring, and evaluating their progress.

The *Crossroads Café* program provides two checklists for learners to use for recording their language learning.

- Learners use the **Student Checklists** found on pages 214–220 of the Worktext to record the number of correct responses to worktext activities.
- Learners use the **Ways to Learn Checklist** found on page 141 of this Teacher's Resource Book to assess their use of learning strategies and to reflect on the ways successful learners manage and monitor their language learning.

Before learners begin a worktext unit, have them turn to the Table of Contents on page iv–v of the Worktext. This page provides an instructional overview, or road map for learners, that identifies the learning strategy and instructional goals for each unit. Learners will appreciate having a sense of where the unit will be taking them. Previewing the content of the unit is in itself an important learning strategy.

Then direct learners' attention to the first page of the unit. After they discuss the title and introductory photo, point out the learning goals and **Ways to Learn** section.

19. MORE ABOUT THE STUDENT CHECKLISTS

It is important for language learners to feel they are making progress. By using the **Student Checklists** (pages 214–220 of Worktext), learners accept responsibility for monitoring their learning. They will not have to ask you how they are doing because they'll know! Help learners establish a regular routine of completing the **Student Checklists**, either in class or at home.

Make sure you review the **Checklists** on a regular basis, too, so you can intervene when necessary. For example, if you notice learners are making few if any errors in one-star activities, encourage them to begin doing both one- and two-star activities. On the other hand, if learners seem to be having difficulty with the three-star activities, encourage them to do only the one- and two-star activities.

20. WHY IS THE WAYS TO LEARN CHECKLIST IMPORTANT?

In addition to monitoring language progress, *Crossroads Café* enhances learners' awareness of **how** they learn.

Use the **Ways to Learn Checklist** (pages 141 and 142 of this book) to have learners reflect on the ways they used the learning strategy in the unit just completed. Ask learners to share the ways they used the strategy. Encourage learners to refer to the **Ways to Learn Checklist** on a regular basis. Remind them to continue using previously introduced strategies even as they add new ones. As learners progress through the worktexts, they will expand their repertoire of learning strategies.

UNIT 14 LIFE GOES ON

TEACHER'S NOTES AT A GLANCE

	ACTIVITIES	MATERIALS	TIME
CLASS OPENER	◆ play **Story Clip #1** ◆ discussion	TV/VCR	5–10 minutes 5–10 minutes
YOUR NEW LANGUAGE	*Do before worktext* ◆ replay **Word Play** ◆ describing the characters ◆ play **Story Clip #2** ◆ visual dictation ◆ partner work	TV/VCR board TV/VCR, board, paper Handout 14-A Handout 14-B	2–5 minutes 10–15 minutes 15–20 minutes 15–20 minutes 10–15 minutes
IN YOUR COMMUNITY	*Do before worktext* ◆ discussion ◆ categorizing *Do after worktext* ◆ matching (Ext. Act. #1)	board board, paper 3" × 5" cards	10–15 minutes 10–15 minutes 10–15 minutes
READ AND WRITE	◆ discussion	get well cards	10–15 minutes
WHAT DO YOU THINK?	*Do after worktext* ◆ play **Story Clip #3** ◆ reading practice (Ext. Act. #2) ◆ information gap	TV/VCR insurance forms, overhead projector, transparencies Handout 14-C	10–15 minutes 15–20 minutes 10–15 minutes
CULTURE CLIP	*Do before worktext* ◆ replay **Culture Clip** ◆ brainstorming ◆ culture comparison	TV/VCR board Handout 14-D	2–5 minutes 5 minutes 10–15 minutes
EPISODE WRAP UP	◆ discussion	board	5–10 minutes

VIDEO HIGHLIGHTS	
15:37–17:23	**Word Play:** Describing things
5:30–7:56	**Culture Clip:** Hospitals
1:22–2:49	**Story Clip #1:** Rosa calls Crossroads Café from the hospital.
13:11–15:26	**Story Clip #2:** Jamal visits Mr. Brashov in the hospital.
17:27–20:22	**Story Clip #3:** Anna Brashov comes to Crossroads Café.

CLASS OPENER

Before you begin Book B, have learners retell Video 13. Make sure learners remember the ending (Mr. Brashov clutched his chest, fell down, and the paramedics took him to the hospital). If you have a copy of *Photo Stories A,* make a transparency of frame 59 on page 220 and have learners discuss it.

Play Story Clip #1 and use the video technique of *watchers and listeners.*

STORY CLIP #1

TIME CODES: 1:22–2:49   **COUNTER TIMES:**

SCENE: Rosa calls Crossroads Café from the hospital.

FIRST LINE: KATHERINE: Jamal.

LAST LINE: KATHERINE: Let's clean up, then go home and get some rest.

While learners are watching and listening to the video clip, ask them to find the answers to these questions:

> *What are Katherine, Henry, and Jamal waiting for?*
> *Who calls?*
> *What does the caller say?*
> *How does Mr. Brashov feel?*
> *When can Mr. Brashov have visitors?*

Do a hand survey about learners' experiences with hospitals. Ask learners to raise their hands when you ask these questions.

> *How many of you have gone to the hospital because you were sick? In what country did you go to the hospital?*
> *How many of you have visited someone in the hospital? Where were you?*

YOUR NEW LANGUAGE

Replay **Word Play** (15:37–17:23) **before** learners begin this section of the *worktext.* To introduce the language focus do the following:

- Write the names of the video characters on the board.
- Ask learners what they know about the characters—age, physical characteristics, personality, and so on. Write the words learners say under each character's name.
- Circle the words that are adjectives. Tell learners that adjectives are words used to describe things.

After learners have completed this section of the *worktext,* play **Story Clip #2.** There are two activities for this story clip.

STORY CLIP #2

TIME CODES: 13:11–15:26   **COUNTER TIMES:**

SCENE: Jamal visits Mr. Brashov in the hospital.

FIRST LINE: MR. BRASHOV: Ah, Jamal. Thank you for coming.

LAST LINE: JAMAL: Good-bye.

Activity #1

Write these lines from the story clip on the board:

1. Nurse, meet Jamal, one of my most <u>important</u> employees at Crossroads Café.
2. Chicken and rice. Mmmmm...that sounds <u>wonderful</u>. And it smells delicious!
3. You're on a <u>restricted</u> diet.
4. No, the café is doing <u>fine</u>.
5. Jess has made sure that I keep everything in <u>good working</u> order.

Then do the following:

- Ask learners to write the numbers 1 to 6 on a piece of paper.
- **While** learners watch the story clip, have them write the name of the character who says each line.
- When you check learners' responses, call attention to the sentences on the board. Ask learners to identify the adjectives in each line.

Activity #2

Replay Story Clip #2 and use the ***thinking and feeling*** and *freeze frame* video techniques. After each line from **Activity #1** is spoken, freeze the frame. Have learners work with a partner to decide what the character was thinking and/or feeling when the line was spoken. Debrief using ***stand up and share.***

Handout 14-A encourages learners to experiment using descriptive words: too, very, and too _____ to _____. Do the following:

- Make an overhead transparency of the page or draw a facsimile on the chalkboard.
- Point to the words <u>I'm sad</u> and have the learners repeat each word after you.
- Point to another set of words: <u>I'm very worried</u>.
- Point to another set of words: <u>I'm too cold to speak</u>.
- Ask learners to choose partners. Ask them to write as many sentences or questions as they can in 10 minutes (15 minutes if learners need more time). There is one rule! A word that appears once in the collage can only appear once in any sentence or question, but can be used in any number of sentences or questions. Circulate while learners are working together and make sure they are all following the directions.
- When the time limit is up, have learners debrief using ***teams share***.
- Do a small group debriefing by asking each pair to share several sentences with the rest of the class.
- Ask learners what rules they have discovered about describing words (adjectives).

Note: This activity can be used as a game or competition by assigning teams a specific number of sentences to write within a certain time period.

Handout 14-B is a discussion activity. It provides learners with additional practice using descriptive words. Learners work with a partner or small group and take turns asking and answering questions about how they feel and why they feel that way in a variety of situations. Depending on the learners' levels, they will point to the appropriate "face" and say:

- I'm _____ because. . . .
- I'm very _____ because. . . .
- I'm too _____ to _____ because. . . .

When learners have completed this activity, ask each pair or small group to think of one or two additional situations and ask their classmates how they feel in those situations.

IN YOUR COMMUNITY

Before learners complete the *worktext* pages, have a large group discussion about medicine.

- Begin by asking learners how many take medicine when they are sick. Tell them to raise their hands if they do. Ask them the names of the medicines they take and what each medicine is for. Write all of this information on the board. In case learners need memory prods, bring in some real drugs (Tylenol®, Pepto Bismol®, Benedryl®, a prescription drug, a home remedy, etc.)

- When the learners can't add any more words to the board, write these three words at the top or bottom: <u>over-the-counter medicine, prescription drug, home remedy.</u> If possible elicit an example of each from the learners.

- Ask learners to work with a partner to put each of the words on the board in one of the three categories. If writing the words is too difficult or too time-consuming for learners, have them use symbols to distinguish the categories. For example, they might use a triangle for over-the-counter drugs, a square for prescription drugs, and a circle for home remedies.

- Ask learners, "How many of you read the labels on the medicine you take?" Ask, "Has anyone had a bad experience because you didn't (or couldn't) read the label?" Tell the learners that the following pages in the *worktext* will help them practice reading medicine labels.

Extension Activity #1 is a matching game.

- Write the names of drugs on 3" × 5" cards (one drug per card per student). Scramble the cards.

- Write the reasons why people take particular drugs on 3" × 5" cards (one reason per card per student). Scramble the cards.

- Give each learner one drug card and one reason card. Have learners walk around and ask each other questions until all of the drugs and reasons for taking them have been matched.

- Model the questions learners need to ask to find matches. For example:

  Q: *I have a headache. Do you have any aspirin?*
  Q: *My stomach hurts. Do you have any Pepto Bismal®?*

- Debrief learners by reading their matched cards aloud.

If you are on friendly terms with a local pharmacist, he or she may give you "patient instructions" on some common drugs that you could use to make additional reading activities.

READ AND WRITE

After learners have completed the *worktext* pages, share some get well cards with them, both serious and humorous. To do the following small group activity, you'll need at least one card for each group of four learners.

- ♦ Number each card.
- ♦ Have learners copy the chart below on their own papers.

CARD NUMBER	REASONS IT'S HUMOROUS	REASONS IT'S SERIOUS
#1		
#2		
#3		
#4		
#5		
#6		

- ♦ Give one card to each group. The group decides whether the card is serious or humorous and writes the reasons for the group's decisions in the chart.
- ♦ After 2–3 minutes, each group passes its card to the group on its right.
- ♦ Have groups continue passing the cards around until each group has discussed every card.
- ♦ Debrief the groups' decisions in a whole class discussion.
- ♦ End with a class discussion about whether or not people send get well cards in the learners' native countries.

A variation is to have learners, working with a partner or in groups of three, write their own get well cards.

WHAT DO YOU THINK?

After learners have completed this section of the *worktext,* play **Story Clip #3** and use the *behavior study* and *silent viewing* video techniques.

> ## STORY CLIP #3
>
> **TIME CODES:** 17:27–20:22   **COUNTER TIMES:**
>
> **SCENE:** Anna Brashov comes to Crossroads Café.
>
> **FIRST LINE:** KATHERINE: Hi. You can have a seat.
>
> **LAST LINE:** JESS: Good-bye.

Play Story Clip #3 without the sound, and ask learners to pay attention to Anna Brashov. After learners have watched the clip, have a large group discussion about Anna. Ask learners to describe her while you write their descriptive words on the board.

Play the clip again with both picture and sound. Write the names of the characters who met Anna on the board: Katherine, Jess, and Jamal. Have learners work with a partner to discuss what each character thinks about Anna. Debrief using **stand up and share.** End the discussion by asking learners:

> *Why didn't Anna want to visit her father in the hospital?*
> *What was in the envelope Anna gave Jess?*
> *How will Mr. Brashov feel when he finds out about Anna's visit to Crossroads Café?*

Extension Activity #2 is a reading activity. In the video, Mr. Brashov asked Rosa to get some insurance papers for him from the safe. Mr. Jenkins said he couldn't understand his insurance forms.

- Bring in some health insurance forms.
- Make a photocopy for each learner.
- Have learners fill out the forms by working with a partner.

Have a class discussion to find out how many learners have health insurance and how many have to fill out forms. Do a hand survey to find out how many learners belong to health maintenance organizations (HMOs) or are enrolled in preferred provider organizations (PPOs). Learners may also be interested in comparing insurance costs.

Handout 14-C is an information gap on insurance benefits for an HMO.

CULTURE CLIP

Replay Culture Clip (5:30–7:56) before learners complete the exercises in the *worktext* and do the following:

- Write on the board: *A hospital is like a small city.*
- Have the class brainstorm a list of reasons why they think that statement might be true.
- Play the clip.
- Ask learners which reasons on the board were mentioned in the clip.

Handout 14-D provides learners with the opportunity to discuss hospital customs in the United States and their native countries. If learners have not had any personal experiences with hospitals in the United States, have them use the information from this video episode.

A variation is to have learners interview someone outside of class for the United States column and report back to the class.

EPISODE WRAP UP

Discuss the title of this episode.

- Write the title on the board.
- Have learners work with a partner or in a small group to make a list of all of the ways life goes on for the characters in this episode.
- Debrief using **best idea.**

VISUAL DICTATION

HANDOUT 14-A

Directions: Make sentences with these words.

talk	pneumonia	my
delicious	my	to	goodnight
tired	say	hospital
salty	getting	friend	losing
very	$10.00	strict	are
hot	angry	and	speak	sick
friends	watch	today	read
speak	tasteless	the	working	happy
I'm	TV	going	home
a	work	my	I
sad	worried	cold	too	country
overtime	food	expensive	ticket	visit

ASK AND ANSWER

HANDOUT 14-B

Use descriptive words to talk about how you feel in different situations.

♦ Work with a partner or in a small group.
♦ Take turns asking each other the following questions.
♦ Add two more questions on the lines below.
♦ To respond, each person points to a face and then answers using one of the sentences below.

> EXAMPLE: Q: *How do you feel <u>when you work overtime?</u>*
> A: *I feel <u>tired.</u>*
> *I feel <u>very tired.</u>*
> *I feel <u>too tired to walk!</u>*

Ask Your Partner: "How do you feel when you . . .
♦ work overtime?"
♦ lose $20.00?"
♦ get a speeding ticket?"
♦ have a cold?"
♦ argue with a friend?"
♦ visit your native country?"
♦ visit a friend in the hospital?"
♦ lose your keys?"
♦ buy new clothes?"
♦ get a raise?"
♦ _____
♦ _____

Your partner points to the appropriate face and answers the question.

terrific   good   so so

not so good   terrible   angry

INFORMATION GAP

HANDOUT 14-C

PARTNER A

Directions: Look at this chart of health-care benefits. Ask your partner questions to complete the chart.

> EXAMPLE: Q: *How much do I pay for doctor visits?*
> A: *Nothing. There is no charge.*

BENEFIT	COST	BENEFIT	COST
Doctor Visits		Generic Prescription Drugs	$3 each
Outpatient Psychiatric Care	$20 per visit	Non-Generic Prescription Drugs	
Hospital Services		Birth Control Pills	$8 each
In-Area Emergency	$10 per visit	Mail Order Prescription Drugs	
Emergency Ambulance Transportation		Outpatient Substance Abuse Treatment	$20 per visit
Out-of Area Emergency	$0	Nicotine Patches	

PARTNER B

Directions: Look at this chart of health-care benefits. Ask your partner questions to fill in the chart.

> EXAMPLE: Q: *How much do I pay for generic prescription drugs?*
> A: *$3.00 for each.*

BENEFIT	COST	BENEFIT	COST
Doctor Visits	$0	Generic Prescription Drugs	
Outpatient Psychiatric Care		Non-generic Prescription Drugs	$8
Hospital Services	None	Birth Control Pills	
In-Area Emergency		Mail-Order Prescription Drugs	$3
Emergency Ambulance Transportation	None	Outpatient Substance Abuse Treatment	$20 per visit
Out-of-Area Emergency	$0	Nicotine Patches	

CULTURE COMPARISON

HANDOUT 14-D

Think about hospitals in the United States and in your native country.

◆ Answer the questions below.
◆ Write your answers in the chart.
◆ Talk to a partner. Are your answers the same or different?
◆ Share your answers with a small group or the rest of the class.

	IN THE UNITED STATES	IN _____
Is it expensive to go to a hospital?		
Do most people have health insurance?		
Does health insurance pay for all medical care costs?		
Do people know their doctors well?		
Do doctors talk to the family about the sick person?		
Can patients have visitors? How many at a time? How often?		
Can children visit patients?		
Do people bring things to patients when they visit? What?		
Can visitors bring food to patients?		

UNIT 14 LIFE GOES ON

Mr. Brashov had a heart attack. Rosa went to the hospital with him. Now the employees are waiting to hear from Rosa. They are all very nervous and worried.

Finally Rosa calls. Mr. Brashov had a mild heart attack, but now he is out of danger. Everyone wants to visit him at the hospital. But Mr. Brashov cannot have visitors until the next day.

At the hospital, Mr. Brashov is feeling better. He wants to go back to work. Rosa comes to visit. The nurse says, "Mr. Brashov can't have any visitors until tomorrow. The rules are very strict here." But the nurse lets Rosa stay for a few minutes.

Mr. Brashov introduces Rosa to his roommate, Joe Jenkins. Joe Jenkins has heart problems, too. Mr. Jenkins tells Mr. Brashov, "You are a very lucky man. You are in the hospital, but you are alive."

Mr. Brashov argues with his nurse, Brenda. Then Rosa and Mr. Brashov talk about the café. Mr. Brashov is worried, and he wants to close it. Rosa tells Mr. Brashov to take care of himself. The employees will take care of Crossroads Café.

The next day, Rosa opens the café. Soon the other employees come. Rosa tells them what to do. As always, Rosa and Katherine start to argue. Neither of them can work if the other is the boss. Henry is too young to be the boss. Jamal has to take care of his baby, so he cannot be the boss. Then Jess comes. The employees decide he should be the boss. Jess agrees to manage the café until Mr. Brashov returns.

In the hospital, Mr. Brashov complains a lot. Katherine and Henry come to visit. They tell Mr. Brashov about Jess. Jess is a good manager. He has many ideas about how to improve things at the restaurant. But Mr. Brashov is not happy to hear about Jess's ideas. He is worried. Maybe nobody needs him. Everything is fine at the café without him.

When Jamal visits Mr. Brashov, he also talks about Jess. Mr. Brashov is not happy. Jamal brings Mr. Brashov some food from the café. Brenda will not let him eat it. After Jamal leaves, Mr. Brashov is very depressed.

A young woman comes to Crossroads Café. She wants to speak to Jess. Her name is Anna, and she is Mr. Brashov's daughter. She doesn't visit her father in the hospital. She gives Jess a package for him. Then she leaves.

At the hospital, Mr. Brashov continues to feel better, but his roommate, Mr. Jenkins, dies. Mr. Brashov did not know Mr. Jenkins was so sick. He never complained. Mr. Brashov feels very bad because he complains all of the time.

Several days pass. It is late afternoon, and the café is busy. Then the electricity goes out. Nobody knows what to do. Suddenly, they hear Mr. Brashov's voice. He is out of the hospital.

Jess gives Mr. Brashov the package from his daughter, Anna. When Mr. Brashov opens it, he sees a picture of a little girl. It's his granddaughter. Anna never told him about her. Mr. Brashov is very surprised and happy.

UNIT 15 BREAKING AWAY

TEACHER'S NOTES
AT A GLANCE

	ACTIVITIES	MATERIALS	TIME
CLASS OPENER	◆ discussion		5–10 minutes
YOUR NEW LANGUAGE	*Do before worktext* ◆ Replay **Word Play** ◆ think-pair-share *Do after worktext* ◆ Johari Window ◆ play **Story Clip #1**	TV/VCR board Handout 15-A TV/VCR	2–5 minutes 10–15 minutes 15–25 minutes 10–15 minutes
IN YOUR COMMUNITY	*Do after worktext* ◆ interview ◆ design a poster (Ext. Act. #1)	Handout 15-B poster board, paper, markers	15-25 minutes 30-45 minutes
READ AND WRITE	◆ play **Story Clip #2** ◆ reading practice	TV/VCR magazine/newspaper stories	10–15 minutes 15–30 minutes
WHAT DO YOU THINK?	◆ play **Story Clip #3** ◆ sorting	TV/VCR Handout 15-C	10–15 minutes 10–15 minutes
CULTURE CLIP	◆ replay **Culture Clip** ◆ panel discussion ◆ role-play	TV/VCR guests Handout 15-D	10–15 minutes 30–45 minutes 10–15 minutes
EPISODE WRAP UP	◆ *think-pair-share* ◆ discussion	board	10–15 minutes 5 minutes

VIDEO HIGHLIGHTS

8:17–12:13	**Culture Clip:** Intercultural relationships
19:06–21:00	**Word Play:** Talking about likes and dislikes
3:55–6:28	**Story Clip #1:** Henry has dinner with his family
12:53–15:32	**Story Clip #2:** Henry has dinner at Sara's house.
21:23–24:14	**Story Clip #3:** Henry's parents meet Sara's parents at Crossroads Café.

◤ CLASS OPENER

See suggestions on page xii in the Introduction.

YOUR NEW LANGUAGE

Replay **Word Play** (19:06–21:00) **before** learners complete this section of the *worktext*. To introduce the language focus, do the following:

- ◆ Write the names of the Crossroads Café characters on the board.
- ◆ Point to each name and say,

  Henry likes Sara. Jess likes to play chess.

  Rosa likes to wear big earrings. Victor likes to worry. Jamal likes to fix things. What does Katherine like?

- ◆ Have learners do a ***think-pair-share*** about one thing each of the characters *likes*, *likes to do*, *doesn't like*, and *doesn't like to do*.

A variation is to do a *sides* activity about learners' likes and dislikes. Use the suggestions below or make up your own.

- ◆ seasons/weather
- ◆ sports/teams/stars
- ◆ music/types/instruments/artists/songs
- ◆ foods/meals/restaurants
- ◆ movie stars

Handout 15-A is a Johari Window. It provides learners with additional opportunities to practice the language focus. **After** you debrief the pairs, review the likes and dislikes of the learners.

Story Clip #1 shows the reaction of Henry's parents to his news about having dinner at the Grayson's. Use the ***thinking and feeling*** and ***freeze-frame*** video techniques.

STORY CLIP #1

TIME CODES: 3:55–6:28   **COUNTER TIMES:**

SCENE: Henry has dinner with his family.

FIRST LINE: MRS. CHANG: Edward, please use the spoon.

LAST LINE: MRS. CHANG: I hope you're right.

- ◆ Have learners work individually or in pairs.
- ◆ Make two grids on the board like the one shown and have learners copy them on their own papers.
- ◆ Play **Story Clip #1** in two segments.
- ◆ Stop the first segment after Mrs. Chang says, "You'll get your chance Thursday night. I invited the Fongs for dinner."
- ◆ Give learners time to complete the grid.
- ◆ Play the second segment and have learners complete the second grid.

♦ Replay one or both of the segments pausing several times to let learners tell what the characters are thinking or feeling.

	THINKING	FEELING
Henry		
Edward		
Mr. Chang		
Mrs. Chang		

If you have time, have a discussion, based on information in the story clip, about the Changs' likes and dislikes.

IN YOUR COMMUNITY

Handout 15-B is an interview. Learners discuss the businesses they visit in their communities. Debrief the pairs in a large group discussion.

Extension Activity #1 provides learners with opportunities to design poster advertisements for one of the businesses they visit.

♦ Have learners decide how they want to work—individually, in pairs, or in small groups.
♦ Ask learners to select one business they visit and design a poster advertisement for it.
♦ Distribute poster board or 11" x 18" paper and colored markers as necessary.
♦ Decide together what information the posters should include, e.g., name, address, phone, hours.
♦ Display the poster (with learners' permission).

READ AND WRITE

Before learners complete this section of the *worktext,* play **Story Clip 2**. Use the *behavior study* video technique.

> ### STORY CLIP #2
>
> **TIME CODES:** 12:53–15:32   **COUNTER TIMES:**
>
> **SCENE:** Henry has dinner at Sara's house.
>
> **FIRST LINE:** MRS. GRAYSON: Sara, please pass some more potatoes to Henry.
>
> **LAST LINE:** HENRY: I think I'd better leave.

♦ Introduce this clip by asking learners what Mr. Chang said would happen.
♦ Play the clip and discuss whether or not Mrs. Chang's predictions were accurate.
♦ Draw this chart on the board.

CHARACTERS	WHAT THEY SAID	WHAT THEY DID
Henry		
Sara		
Mr. Grayson		
Mrs. Grayson		

- ◆ Play the clip again and ask learners to comment on what people said and how they acted.

Collect newspaper or magazine stories about prejudice, intercultural, or interracial issues and bring them to class for additional reading, writing, and discussion practice. Encourage learners to do the same.

WHAT DO YOU THINK?

The characters in this video not only share a lot of opinions, they make a lot of inferences. Unfortunately, inferences are not necessarily true.

Before learners complete this section of the *worktext,* play **Story Clip #3.**

STORY CLIP #3

TIME CODES: 21:23–24:14   **COUNTER TIMES:**

SCENE: Henry invites his parents and the Graysons to a meeting at Crossroads Café.

FIRST LINE: HENRY TO KATHERINE AND ROSA: What do you think?

LAST LINE: MR. CHANG: I think you're right.

- ◆ Write FACTS and INFERENCES on the board.
- ◆ Play the clip twice. The first time, learners write 3–5 facts. The second time, learners write 3–5 inferences.
- ◆ Have learners share their FACTS and INFERENCES with a partner.
- ◆ Each pair chooses one FACT and one INFERENCE to share with the class.

Handout 15-C is a sorting activity. Learners distinguish facts from inferences.

CULTURE CLIP

Replay **Culture Clips** (8:17–12:13) **before** learners complete this section of the *worktext.* If possible, invite some teenagers to class for a panel discussion on intercultural, interfaith, and interracial relationships. Try to include both males and females. To prepare for the panel discussion, have learners brainstorm a list of questions they would like the teenagers to discuss.

- ◆ Make copies of the questions.
- ◆ Give copies to the teenagers.

- Have a class discussion to determine the format of the panel discussion.
- Select one or more learners to be M.C.s (master of ceremony a la Ricki Lake, Sally Jessy Raphael, Jenny Jones, etc.)
- Explain the format to the teenagers.

As a follow-up to the panel discussion, have learners write thank-you notes.

A variation is to have learners role-play the teenagers. Ask them to role-play a role they might not agree with.

Handout 15-D provides learners with opportunities to role-play Crossroads Café characters who have different points of view about the events in this episode. Have learners work in groups of three. Two learners do the role-play while the third learner observes and takes notes about the facts and opinions heard. Learners can do this several times so that each person has a chance to be the observer.

▶ EPISODE WRAP UP

After learners have completed this section of the *worktext*, have a discussion about the title of the video.

- Write BREAKING AWAY on the board.
- Have learners do a ***think-pair-share***. Use these questions or make up your own.

  Which characters are breaking away?
  What are they breaking away from?

- Debrief the pairs and conclude the discussion by asking learners to share any stories they might have about breaking away.

SAME OR DIFFERENT

HANDOUT 15-A

Work with a partner. One person is **A** and the other is **B**. Work together to complete the grid below.

- In the *top left-hand box*, write **three** things you both like and **three** things you both like to do.
- In the *top right-hand box*, write **three** things A likes but B doesn't and **three** things A likes to do but B doesn't.
- In the bottom *left-hand box*, write **three** things B likes but A doesn't and **three** things B likes to do but A doesn't.
- In the bottom *right-hand box*, write **three** things neither of you like and **three** things neither of you like to do.

BOTH A AND B	**ONLY A**
Like	Likes
Like to do	Likes to do
Likes	Like
Likes to do	Like to do

ONLY B	**NEITHER A NOR B**

INTERVIEW

HANDOUT 15-B

There is a new business next to Crossroads Café. What businesses are in your communities? Which ones do you go to?

- ◆ Interview a partner about businesses in his or her community.
- ◆ Ask the questions below.
- ◆ Write the answers in the chart.
- ◆ Talk about the questions below the chart with your partner.
- ◆ Share your answers with another pair.

NAME:	INTERVIEWER:		
What businesses do you go to in your community?	What are the names of the businesses?	Why do you go there?	How often do you go there?
1.			
2.			
3.			
4.			
5.			
6.			

Do you go to any of these businesses? _____

Which ones? _____

Which businesses do you like? Why? Why do you think they are successful?

_____

_____

CATEGORIES

HANDOUT 15-C

FACT: Crossroads Café is a restaurant. INFERENCE: Crossroads Café is busy because the food is good. What's the difference between a fact and an inference?

- ◆ Work with a partner or a small group.
- ◆ Write two more FACTS and INFERENCES on the blank cards.
- ◆ Cut the cards on the lines.
- ◆ Scramble the cards and put them face down in a pile.
- ◆ Take turns. Each person picks up a card, reads it, and decides if it is a FACT or an INFERENCE.
- ◆ Put the FACTS in one column and the INFERENCES in another.
- ◆ Share your answers with another pair or group.

✄ -

FACTS	INFERENCES
Victor Brashov is the owner of Crossroads Café.	Victor Brashov is too old to run a business.
Henry and Sara are 17-year olds.	Sara cares about Henry more than Henry cares about Sara.
Rosa is a cook.	Henry doesn't respect his parents.
Linda Blasco owns a laundromat.	Linda's laundromat will bring more customers to Crossroads Café.
Mr. and Mrs. Chang want Henry to date Chinese girls.	Both the Changs and the Graysons are prejudiced.
Edward wants to meet Karen Fong.	The Changs and the Graysons think Henry and Sara will get married.
Mr. and Mrs. Grayson went to Hong Kong.	Linda Blasco has good business sense.

ROLE-PLAY

HANDOUT 15-D

In this episode, everyone had a lot of opinions.

- ◆ Work with a partner.
- ◆ Read the situations below.
- ◆ Role-play one or more of the conversations or create your own role-play. Write it on the blank card.
- ◆ Share your role-play with the class.

Henry tells his mother about his dinner at the Graysons.	Mr. and Mrs. Chang talk about what happened at Crossroads Café.
Henry asks Jamal for advice.	Jamal tells Jihan what happened between Henry and Sara.
Rosa gives Henry advice.	Edward tells Henry about dinner with Mr. and Mrs. Fong.
Henry talks to Jess about intercultural dating.	Victor tells Nicolae about his new neighbor.
Sara talks to Henry after their parents meet at Crossroads Café.	Jess tells Carol about Victor's new neighbor.
Mr. and Mrs. Grayson talk about Henry after he leaves their house.	

UNIT 15 BREAKING AWAY

There are workmen in the vacant building next to Crossroads Café. Mr. Brashov is happy about the new business because vacant buildings are bad for business.

Sara, Henry's girlfriend, comes in the café. Sara says to Henry, "Did you tell them, yet?" Henry finally says, "Sara and I are going together." But nobody is surprised. They already knew.

Sara wants to tell her parents and Henry's parents that they are going together. Henry doesn't think that's necessary. Sara disagrees. She invites Henry to have dinner at her house on Thursday with her parents.

Henry is eating dinner with his parents. His mother has some news. Old friends, the Fongs, are moving back to town. Their daughter, Karen, is the same age as Henry. Karen and Henry played together when they were young. The Fongs are coming for dinner on Thursday night.

Henry says, "I'm having dinner at Sara's on Thursday." Henry's mother tells him to prepare for disappointment. Sara's parents will be unhappy because Henry is Chinese. Henry disagrees with his mother.

Jamal has news for Mr. Brashov. The new business next door is a laundromat. Mr. Brashov doesn't like this news. He thinks a laundromat will be bad for business. People will come to Crossroads Café for change for the laundry machines, not for food.

Rosa suddenly says, "No water!" At the same time, a woman comes in and asks for change for the pay phone. Her name is Linda, and she is the owner of the laundromat. Linda wants to call the Water and Power Company. Her workmen cannot turn off the water to install the washing machines. Mr. Brashov tells her, "Your workmen turned off my water."

It's Thursday night. Henry is having dinner at the Graysons. First, Mr. Grayson talks about football. Henry hates the Graysons' favorite team. Then Henry talks about hockey. The Graysons are not hockey fans. Next, the Graysons talk about food. This is not a good topic either. Finally Henry says, "Sara and I are going together." This is definitely a bad topic.

Sara's mother asks Henry and Sara to wait for a while. Henry thinks Sara's parents don't approve of him. He gets up from the table and leaves the Grayson home.

There are problems at Crossroads Café, too. Mr. Brashov is angry about his new neighbor again. Now her workmen are repainting the lines in the parking lot.

Henry is very sad. He tells Jamal about his dinner at the Graysons and his problems with Sara. Rosa overhears the discussion. Rosa and Katherine give Henry advice. Henry decides to invite his parents, Sara, and her parents to Crossroads Café to talk.

The Changs and the Graysons are at Crossroads Café. Henry apologizes to the Graysons for his rude behavior. Mr. and Mrs. Grayson explain their feelings about Henry and Sara. They talk about their plans for their daughter's future. After a lot of discussion, all of the parents agree to trust their children.

Mr. Brashov decides he likes his new neighbor after all. Linda's workmen made six new parking places—three for him and three for her.

UNIT 16 THE BOTTOM LINE

TEACHER'S NOTES
AT A GLANCE

	ACTIVITIES	MATERIALS	TIME
CLASS OPENER	♦ discussion		5–10 minutes
YOUR NEW LANGUAGE	*Do before worktext* ♦ replay **Word Play** ♦ discussion ♦ language practice ♦ role-play (Ext. Act. #1)	TV/VCR board Handout 16-A board	2–5 minutes 5–10 minutes 15–20 minutes 15–20 minutes
IN YOUR COMMUNITY	*Do before worktext* ♦ roundrobin *Do after worktext* ♦ play **Story Clip #1** ♦ information gap	board TV/VCR Handout 16-B	10–15 minutes 10–15 minutes 10–15 minutes
READ AND WRITE	*Do after worktext* ♦ discussion ♦ make flyers	newspapers paper, markers	10–15 minutes 30–45 minutes
WHAT DO YOU THINK?	*Do after worktext* ♦ play **Story Clips 2a and 2b** ♦ sorting & discussion ♦ reading and discussion (Ext. Act. #2)	TV/VCR Handout 16-C direct mail ads	10–15 minutes 10–15 minutes 10–15 minutes
CULTURE CLIP	♦ replay **Culture Clip** ♦ sides activity ♦ interview	TV/VCR Handout 16-D	2–5 minutes 5–10 minutes 15–20 minutes
EPISODE WRAP UP	♦ discussion	board	5–10 minutes

VIDEO HIGHLIGHTS	
15:29–17:12	**Word Play:** Reporting information
8:53–11:02	**Culture Clip:** Aging
4:22–5:21	**Story Clip #1:** Mr. Brashov meets with Mr. Littleton at the bank.
12:55–14:17	**Story Clip #2a:** Mr. Littleton makes his first visit to the café.
22:37–24:13	**Story Clip #2b:** Mr. Littleton makes his second visit to the café.

CLASS OPENER

See suggestions on page xii of the Introduction.

YOUR NEW LANGUAGE

Replay **Word Play** (15:29–17:12) before learners complete this section of the *worktext*. To introduce the language focus, do the following.

♦ Write these questions on the board:

> *What did you do yesterday?*
> *Who did you talk to?*
> *What did you talk about?*

♦ Have learners interview a partner and write the answers to the questions on the board.

♦ Ask for some volunteers to answer the questions about their partners while you write sentences like these on the board.

> _____ *said his partner went to work.*
> *He told me his partner talked to some friends at lunch.*
> _____ *said they discussed their performance reviews.*

♦ Continue writing sentences on the board until you feel learners understand how to report information.

♦ Ask for more volunteers to orally report information from the interviews.

Handout 16-A provides learners with opportunities to practice the language used for reporting information. **Before** learners do the handout, review the two ways of reporting information from the *worktext*. Write one example of each on the board for learners to use as examples or tell learners to turn to the **Your New Language** pages while they are doing the handout.

Extension Activity #1 is a role-play that provides learners with additional practice reporting information.

♦ Write the names of the Crossroads Café characters on the board.

♦ Ask each learner to choose one character and write five questions she'd like to ask that character.

♦ Have learners work in groups of three.

♦ One learner reads her questions to the group.

♦ Another learner answers the questions.

♦ The third learner reports what the second learner said.

♦ Ask for volunteers to share their role-plays with the class.

IN YOUR COMMUNITY

Before learners complete this section of the worktext, do a **roundrobin** about loans.

♦ Write the word LOAN on the board.

♦ Ask learners to brainstorm about loans—types of loans, where to get loans, what things people get loans for.

♦ Write the responses on the board.

♦ Sort them into categories using different symbols for each category. For example, put a star next to words related to places to get loans or put a triangle next to words related to reasons for loans.

♦ Have learners copy the categories on their papers.

◆ End the discussion by asking learners if they have any "loan stories" they'd like to share with the class.

Banks are just one place to get loans. Find out if anyone in the class belongs to a credit union. Explain what a credit union is before learners complete **Handout 16-B**—an information gap about interest rates for loans at a credit union.

After learners have completed this section of the *worktext,* play **Story Clip #1** and use the *thinking and feeling* video technique.

STORY CLIP #1

TIME CODES: 4:22–5:21   **COUNTER TIMES:**

SCENE: Mr. Brashov meets with Mr. Littleton at the bank.

FIRST LINE: LITTLETON: Come in.

LAST LINE: LITTLETON: If you know what I mean?

◆ Draw the chart below on the board.

MR. LITTLETON		MR. BRASHOV	
THINKING	FEELING	THINKING	FEELING

◆ Ask learners to copy the chart on their papers.
◆ Have learners take notes about what each character is thinking and feeling while they are watching the clip.
◆ Replay the clip as necessary.
◆ Have learners work with a partner to compare notes.
◆ Debrief in a large group discussion.

▶ READ & WRITE

After learners have completed this section of the *worktext,* have a discussion about companies that have tried to cut expenses by downsizing. Ask learners to raise their hands if they . . .

◆ know of any companies downsizing in their communities?
◆ know any people who have lost their jobs because of downsizing?
◆ are worried about losing their jobs?
◆ are looking for new jobs because they are worried?

A variation is to play a news clip from TV or radio about a company that is downsizing or have learners bring in some stories from the newspaper to share with the class.

Extension Activity #1 provides learners with an opportunity to design flyers for Crossroads Café.

◆ Divide learners into pairs or small groups of three.
◆ Distribute paper and colored markers, crayons, or pencils to each group.
◆ Tell learners to design a flyer for Crossroads Café. They can use Rosa's idea for a two-for-one special or any idea they have.
◆ Have learners share their flyers with the rest of the class.

WHAT DO YOU THINK?

After learners have completed the pages in the *worktext,* play **Story Clips #2a and #2b.** Learners compare and contrast Mr. Littleton's two visits to Crossroads Café.

STORY CLIP #2A

TIME CODES: 12:55–14:17   **COUNTER TIMES:**

SCENE: Mr. Littleton makes his first visit to the café.

FIRST LINE: MR. BRASHOV: This is amazing.

LAST LINE: MR. LITTLETON: I'll be expecting to hear from you.

STORY CLIP #2B

TIME CODES: 22:37–24:13   **COUNTER TIMES:**

SCENE: Mr. Littleton makes his second visit to the café.

FIRST LINE: HARRY: G-twenty-seven.

LAST LINE: MR. LITTLETON: If you can keep this up we might consider giving you a loan after all.

♦ Draw the following chart on the board and ask learners to copy it on their papers.

MR. LITTLETON'S FIRST VISIT	MR. LITTLETON'S SECOND VISIT
What Seniors Are Doing	What Seniors Are Doing
What Mr. Littleton Says	What Mr. Littleton Says

♦ Ask learners to take notes about what the seniors are doing during each of the visits and what Mr. Littleton says at the conclusion of each visit.
♦ Play the clips as many times as necessary.
♦ Have learners work in groups of three or four member to compare their notes.
♦ Debrief using ***teams share.***

Handout 16-C is a sorting and discussion activity. Learners discuss ways for Mr. Brashov to increase the number of customers and profits and sort them into ideas he should consider and ideas he should ignore.

Extension Activity #2 is a discussion about direct mail. Many local businesses such as dentists, car repair shops, restaurants, and carpet cleaning services attempt to attract new customers using the mail. Collect examples of direct mail advertising. Then do the following.

♦ Divide learners into mixed-ability groups of three or four members.
♦ Give each group 3-to-5 pieces of direct mail advertising.

- Write these questions on the board and have learners answer them for each ad they have.

> *What product is being advertised? Where is this place?*
> *Do you know anybody who has used a coupon like this?*
> *What happened? Were they satisfied or dissatisfied?*
> *Would you use this coupon? Why or why not?*
> *Do you think this coupon is a good way to attract more customers? Why or why not?*
> *What else can this business do to get new customers?*

- Have each group share its best ad with the rest of the class.

If possible, invite someone connected to direct mail—a printer or advertiser—to class to talk about this way of attracting new customers. Have learners write their questions and practice them before the interview.

CULTURE CLIP

Replay **Culture Clip** (8:53–11:02) **before** learners complete this section of the *worktext*. **While** learners watch the clip, ask them to make a list of all of the different things the senior citizens talk about (what they do). **After** the clip, have learners discuss with a partner the things they think they will do when they are senior citizens.

If there is time, have a class discussion about issues related to senior citizens. Try a *sides activity* to get the discussion started. Use these questions or make up your own.

> *Seniors have better lives in the United States than in my native country.*
> *Seniors are not as respected in the United States as they are in my native country.*
> *Seniors have more money to spend than younger people.*
> *Seniors think about their health too much.*
> *People over the age of 75 shouldn't be allowed to drive cars.*
> *People over the age of 72 shouldn't be allowed to work, because they take jobs away from younger people.*

Handout 16-D is an interview. If there is time, **after** learners have completed the handout, have a discussion about famous senior citizens from around the world. Brainstorm a list of these seniors and suggest learners bring in stories from the newspapers about them.

Extension Activity #3 is an interview of a senior citizen.

- Invite a senior citizen to class.
- Have the learners prepare questions to ask before the interview, so the senior knows what to expect.
- After the interview, ask learners to write thank-you notes to the senior.

EPISODE WRAP UP

Before learners complete **Check Your English**, have a discussion about the title of this episode.

- Write the title on the board.
- Ask learners what a bottom line is. Accept any examples that come close to the meaning and write them on the board.

REPORTING INFORMATION

HANDOUT 16-A

Mr. Brashov had a meeting with a banker to talk about a loan. He told Jess about the meeting.

♦ Work with a partner.
♦ Each person write five questions on the blank cards below.
♦ Ask each other the questions and write the answers on your own paper.
♦ Work with another pair.
♦ Take turns reading each other the questions and reporting what your partner said.
♦ Use the two ways to report information from the *worktext*.

✂ -

INFORMATION GAP

HANDOUT 16-B

PARTNER A

Mr. Brashov went to a bank for a loan. But there are other places to get loans, too. With a partner look at these loan rates for a credit union.

♦ Ask and answer questions to find the missing information.

EXAMPLE: A: *What is the interest rate for a 12-month personal loan?*
B: *It's 11.25% APR.**

♦ Write the information in the blanks.

LOAN RATES			
Personal loans		Auto Loans - Used Cars	
12 months		100% -1 year old/60 months	
24 months	12.75%	90% - 2 years old/48 months	8.75%
25–36 months		90% -3 years old/42 months	
Auto Loans - New Cars		Home Equity Loans	
100% - 48 months	8.00%	60 months Fixed Rate	7.50%
100% - 60 months		120 months Fixed Rate	
90% - 72 months	8.50%	180 months Variable Rate	Prime

* APR-Annual Percentage Rate

 -

PARTNER B

Mr. Brashov went to a bank for a loan. But there are other places to get loans, too. With a partner look at these loan rates for a credit union.

♦ Ask and answer questions to find the missing information.

EXAMPLE: B: *What is the interest rate for a 24-month personal loan?*
A: *It's 12.75% APR.**

♦ Write the information in the blanks.

LOAN RATES			
Personal loans		Auto Loans - Used Cars	
12 months	11.75%	100% -1 year old/60 months	8.25%
24 months		90% - 2 years old/48 months	
25–36 months	13.75%	90% -3 years old/42 months	8.75%
Auto Loans - New Cars		Home Equity Loans	
100% - 48 months		60 months Fixed Rate	
100% - 60 months	8.25%	120 months Fixed Rate	Call
90% - 72 months		180 months Variable Rate	

* APR-Annual Percentage Rate

SOLVE THE PROBLEM

HANDOUT 16-C

Mr. Brashov needs to improve his profits. In other words, he needs to make more money.

- ◆ Work with a partner or a small group.
- ◆ Read the ideas on the cards to help increase Mr. Brashov's profits.
- ◆ Write one or two more ideas on the blank cards.
- ◆ Together decide which ideas Mr. Brashov should use and which ideas he should ignore. Put them in two piles.
- ◆ Share your good ideas with the rest of the class. Explain why your ideas are good.

✂ ---

Stay open longer hours.	Serve gourmet food and special drinks like espresso or latte.
Fire Jamal.	Redecorate.
Fire Henry.	Charge one price for breakfast meals, one price for lunches, and so on.
Reduce the number of items on the menu.	Advertise more and offer discounts to regular customers.
Serve only healthy foods—no salt, no fat, no sugar.	Offer senior citizen discounts.

INTERVIEW

HANDOUT 16-D

Jess surprises Mr. Brashov when he joins a group at the Senior Citizens' Center. Mr. Brashov wants to know why Jess wants to be with old people.

♦ Interview a partner about senior citizens.
♦ Write your partner's answers on the lines below.
♦ Share your interview with the rest of the class.

NAME: **INTERVIEWER:**

1. To a 10-year old, 25 is old. What age is old to you?

2. How will you know when you are old?

3. Jess is retired. When do you plan to retire?

4. What do you plan to do when you retire?

5. Who do you think is older—Mr. Brashov or Jess? Why?

6. Who is the oldest person you know? How old is this person?

7. Does this person act old? Why or why not?

8. Does this person have any problems because of his or her age?

9. What are they? What are some things senior citizens shouldn't do?

10. Many people over 75 years old live in retirement homes. Where will you live when you are 75?

UNIT 16 THE BOTTOM LINE

It's lunchtime on a snowy, winter day. The employees at Crossroads Café are unhappy. The stove is not working, and there are very few customers.

Mr. Brashov is very worried about the stove, and he is angry, too. Jamal tries to fix the stove, but it is very old and needs a new part. Mr. Brashov says, "Maybe I need a new handyman." Jamal's feelings are very hurt.

Jess comes to the café. He usually comes in every day, but yesterday he didn't come. Jess joined a group at the Senior Citizens' Center. Now he plays chess there every morning.

Jess knows about the trouble with the stove. He tells Mr. Brashov to buy a new one. Mr. Brashov has a meeting tomorrow at a bank. He is going to apply for a loan to buy a new stove. Jess gives him advice about how to talk to the banker.

The next day Mr. Brashov goes to the bank. He follows Jess's advice, but it doesn't help. Mr. Littleton, the banker, thinks Mr. Brashov's expenses are too high. He will not approve a loan unless Mr. Brashov cuts his daily costs. One way to do this is to lay off some employees. Mr. Brashov needs to make more money if he wants a loan.

Later at the café, the employees want to know what happened at the bank. Mr. Brashov tells them. They discuss ways to get more customers, so Mr. Brashov can make more money. Henry offers to make flyers for a lunch special. He will put them around the neighborhood.

The next day, Crossroads Café has many customers. Mr. Brashov thanks Henry. But Henry didn't deliver any flyers. He overslept. Jess brought his group from the Senior Citizens' Center to the café for their morning coffee break.

Mr. Littleton from the bank enters the café. At first he is happy to see so many customers. Then he notices something. People are not eating. They are talking, reading the newspaper, playing cards, and sleeping. This is not the way to make more money. He tells Mr. Brashov to make changes fast!

Jess is in Mr. Brashov's office. Mr. Brashov is very sad. He is worried about the café and about the bank loan. Mr. Brashov tells Jess, "The banker thinks I am a fool. He will never give me a loan."

Nobody can find Jamal. Mr. Brashov was angry with Jamal because he couldn't fix the stove. Now Jamal hasn't come to work for two days. The employees wonder, "Is Jamal sick? Is he looking for a new job?"

Jess has another idea for a way to help Mr. Brashov. His seniors group will have lunch and play Bingo at Crossroads Café on Thursday. This time, everybody will order food!

When Mr. Littleton makes another surprise visit to Crossroads Café, he is happy to see so many customers eating. Maybe he will give Mr. Brashov a loan to buy a new stove.

Then Jamal comes to work. He is very dirty, but he is happy. He went to every junkyard in town, and he finally found the part to fix the stove. Mr. Brashov won't need a loan from the bank after all!

UNIT 17 UNITED WE STAND

TEACHER'S NOTES
AT A GLANCE

	ACTIVITIES	MATERIALS	TIME
CLASS OPENER	◆ discussion		5–10 minutes
YOUR NEW LANGUAGE	*Do before worktext* ◆ replay **Word Play** ◆ discussion *Do after worktext* ◆ play **Story Clip #1** ◆ matching ◆ making complaints (Ext. Act. #1)	TV/VCR board TV/VCR Handout 17-A paper	2–5 minutes 5–10 minutes 10–15 minutes 15–20 minutes 10–15 minutes
IN YOUR COMMUNITY	◆ reading practice ◆ play **Story Clip #2** ◆ 3-step interview ◆ information gap	leases TV/VCR board Handout 17-B	10–15 minutes 5–10 minutes 10–15 minutes 10–15 minutes
READ AND WRITE	◆ hand survey/discussion ◆ reading practice—BINGO	 Handout 17-C	5 minutes 15–20 minutes
WHAT DO YOU THINK?	◆ play **Story Clip #3** ◆ discussion	TV/VCR paper	5–10 minutes 5–10 minutes
CULTURE CLIP	◆ replay **Culture Clip** ◆ discussion ◆ problem-solving	TV/VCR Handout 17-D	2–5 minutes 5–10 minutes 15–20 minutes
EPISODE WRAP UP	◆ discussion	board	5–10 minutes

VIDEO HIGHLIGHTS	
18:27–20:10	**Word Play:** Making complaints
6:16–8:40	**Culture Clip:** Tenants and landlord rights and responsibilities
14:13–15:20	**Story Clip #1:** A man comes to Crossroads Café to collect Rosa's rent.
15:22–15:59	**Story Clip #2:** The employees at Crossroads Café encourage Rosa to organize a tenants' rights meeting.
16:23–18:25	**Story Clip #3:** Rosa invites the tenants of her building to a meeting at Crossroads Café.

CLASS OPENER

See suggestions on page xii in the Introduction.

YOUR NEW LANGUAGE

Replay **Word Play** (18:27–20:10) **before** learners begin this section in the *worktext*.
There are subtle differences between stating problems and making complaints that may make this section difficult for learners. For example, "The garbage is spilling over" is a problem, but adding "There are not enough garbage cans" makes it a complaint.

To introduce the language focus:

- Write on the board a list of problems learners have with their homes or apartments.
- Ask, "Have you ever complained about any of these problems? Which ones?"
- Ask volunteers to share information with the class about their problems, what they did, who they complained to, and what the outcome was.

After learners have completed the pages in the *worktext,* play **Story Clip #1.**

STORY CLIP #1

TIME CODES: 14:13–15:20   **COUNTER TIMES:**

SCENE: A man comes to Crossroads Café to collect Rosa's rent check.

FIRST LINE: KATHERINE: Sorry, we're closed.

LAST LINE: MAN: Thank you Ms. Rivera.

- Use the ***roundtable*** or ***roundrobin*** technique to have learners make a list of all of the problems mentioned in the clip.
- Have learners compare their lists with a partner or a small group.
- Play the clip again.
- Have the pairs or groups write solutions to the problems using the video and adding their own ideas.
- Debrief using ***teams share***.

Handout 17-A is a matching activity for pairs, small groups, or a whole class. A variation is to play a memory game like concentration with the cards.

Extension Activity #1

Many of the characters in Crossroads Café complain about things or each other. This activity is a good way for you to check learners' familiarity with the characters. Try the following.

- Write characters' names on the board.
- Have learners work with a partner to write one complaint, real or imagined, for each character.
- When they have finished writing complaints, have the pairs share their complaints with another pair.
- Ask small groups of four learners to decide which complaints (for each character) they like the best and share them with rest of the class.

Rental agreements are hard for everyone to understand! For additional practice reading leases:

♦ Collect several leases from learners to share with the class.

♦ Make copies of the leases and distribute them. Edit the leases to the learners' comprehension levels by giving the easiest leases to the lowest level learners.

♦ Have learners work with partners to answer the questions in the *worktext* about the new lease.

After learners have completed the pages in the *worktext,* play **Story Clip #2.** Use the *culture comparison* video technique.

STORY CLIP #2

TIME CODES: 15:22–15:59   **COUNTER TIMES:**

SCENE: The employees at Crossroads Café encourage Rosa to organize a tenants' rights meeting.

FIRST LINE: KATHERINE: Rosa, you're not going to give up, are you?

LAST LINE: ROSA: How can I say no? All right . . . let's do it!

♦ Write these questions on the board.

Do tenants have meetings to solve problems in your country?

Are they successful? Why or why not?

Have you ever attended a tenants' rights meeting? If yes, what happened?

Would your coworkers in the United States or in your native country encourage you to organize a tenants' rights group? Why or why not?

Would your boss in the United States or in your native country let you have a tenants' rights meeting at your workplace? Why or why not?

♦ Tell learners to think about the questions while they watch the story clip.

♦ Then have learners do *three-step interviews* to discuss the questions.

♦ Debrief in a large class discussion.

HANDOUT 17-B is an information gap. It familiarizes learners with some commonly used abbreviations and provides opportunities for learners to practice spelling and clarification.

♦ For the first game, all of the learners should have BINGO at the same time.

♦ For a second game, give learners blank BINGO forms and have them copy abbreviations from the board any where on their BINGO forms. Play until several people earn BINGO.

READ AND WRITE

Before learners have completed the pages in the *worktext,* do a hand survey about complaints learners have had or have made in the past six months or year. Ask questions like the following or make up your own. Tell learners to raise their hands if they . . .

> *Had a housing complaint? Called to complain? Wrote to complain? Complained in person?*
>
> *Had a complaint about something they bought? Called to complain? Wrote to complain? Complained in person?*
>
> *Had a complaint about a bill they paid? Called to complain? Wrote to complain? Complained in person?*

If learners had complaints, but did not do anything, ask them to explain why.

HANDOUT 17-C is a BINGO game. It provides learners with additional practice in reading abbreviations used in classified ads. Most newspapers print a legend of the abbreviations they use. You can use that to select the abbreviations you want for a second BINGO game.

WHAT DO YOU THINK?

After learners have completed the pages in the *worktext,* play **Story Clip #3.** Use the *freeze frame* video technique at the beginning of the scene to focus learners' attentions on the tenants' signs. Have learners read the signs aloud.

While learners are watching the clip, have them make a list of things the tenants decide to do. Play the clip again. After learners share their lists with partners, debrief in a large group discussion. On the board, write the tenants suggestions. Ask learners if they agree or disagree with the tenants.

STORY CLIP #3

TIME CODES: 16:23–18:25   **COUNTER TIMES:**

SCENE: Rosa invites the tenants of her building to a meeting at Crossroads Café.

FIRST LINE: ROSA: Can I have your attention please?

LAST LINE: MORE TENANTS: No water, no rent.

CULTURE CLIP

Replay **Culture Clip** (6:16–8:40) before learners complete the pages in the *worktext*. *Freeze frame* the scenes that show problems and ask learners to describe what they see. **HANDOUT 17-D is** a problem-solving activity. This activity ask learners to think about the problems they have at home and make decisions about how to solve them. It also provides learners with an opportunity to share their expertise or knowledge with each other. **Before** learners do this exercise, write the example below on the board.

PROBLEM: THE WATER IN MY BATHROOM SINK WON'T GO DOWN THE DRAIN.		
PROBLEM	HOW TO SOLVE	COST
The water doesn't go down the drain.	Call a plumber.	$50–100.
	Use a plunger.	free (if have already)
	Pour Draino® or Liquid Plumber® down the drain.	$5.00
	Ask a friend for advice.	free

EPISODE WRAP UP

After learners have completed the *worktext* pages, have a discussion about the title of this video.

♦ Write the title on the board.
♦ Ask learners,

  What does united mean?
  Who was united in this episode?

♦ Ask,

  Can anyone think of some real-life examples of the title?

MATCHING

HANDOUT 17-A

Work with a partner or a small group to match problems and complaints with solutions.

♦ Add two more complaints and solutions to the blank cards.
♦ Cut out the cards.
♦ Scramble them.
♦ Take turns reading the cards aloud.
♦ Match the problems or complaints with the solutions.
♦ Try to think of additional solutions for as many cards as you can.
♦ Share your solutions with the class.

PROBLEMS/COMPLAINTS	SOLUTIONS
Your paycheck has a mistake.	Tell your boss.
Your oven doesn't get hot.	Call an appliance repair person.
Your car won't start.	Call a service station.
Your phone doesn't work.	Ask a neighbor to use her phone.
A store advertised a CD player for $79.00, but the store doesn't have any in stock.	Ask for a raincheck.
Your car insurance increased $200.	Check into prices at other insurance companies.
The water in your toilet won't go down.	Call a plumber.
The milk you just bought is spoiled.	Return it and ask for a new gallon.

INFORMATION GAP

HANDOUT 17-B

PARTNER A

Directions: You are looking for a new apartment. The ads in the newspaper have many abbreviations. Ask your partner what the abbreviations mean. Complete the chart below.

> EXAMPLE: A: *What does* **dlx** *mean?*
> B: *It means* **deluxe.**
> A: *Can you spell that?*
> B: *Yes. d e l u x e.*

ABBREVIATION	WORD	ABBREVIATION	WORD
dlx		ht	heat
BR	bedroom	nr shpg	
incl		x-ways	expressways
appls	appliances	lrg	
prkg		a/c	air conditioning
sec	security	lndry facil	

PARTNER B

Directions: You are looking for a new apartment. The ads in the newspaper have many abbreviations. Ask your partner what the abbreviations mean. Complete the chart below.

> EXAMPLE: B: *What does* **ht** *mean?*
> A: *It means* **heat.**
> B: *Can you spell that?*
> A: *Yes. h e a t.*

ABBREVIATION	WORD	ABBREVIATION	WORD
dlx	deluxe	ht	
BR		nr shpg	near shopping
incl	including	x-ways	
appls		lrg	large
prkg	parking	a/c	
sec		lndry facil	laundry facilities

BINGO

HANDOUT 17-C

B	I	N	G	O
AVL	DR	FLR	IMMAC	PVT
BA(S)	DIN RM	FRPL	KIT	REF
BLDG	D/W	**FREE SPACE**	LVG RM	SCHL
CPTG	ELEC	GAR	MO	STV
CRNR	ELEV	HW HT	NR	UTIL

Crossroads Café   United We Stand

PROBLEM-SOLVING

HANDOUT 17-D

Everyone's home has problems.

♦ Make a list on the lines below of some problems in your home.
♦ Choose five problems and write them in the chart.
♦ Decide who can fix or solve each problem.
♦ Guess how much money it will cost to fix the problem (not all problems cost money to fix).
♦ Share your list with a partner or a small group and discuss the problems. Are your problems the same or different?
♦ Do your classmates agree with how much it will cost to fix the problems?

PROBLEMS: _____

_____

_____

_____

_____

_____

_____

_____

PROBLEMS	HOW TO SOLVE	COST, IF ANY?

UNIT 17 UNITED WE STAND

Rosa is late for work. She is having problems with the water in her apartment. She has green cream on her face, and there is no water to wash her face. Finally, she cleans her face with mouthwash.

At Crossroads Café, Mr. Brashov is worried about Rosa because she is late. The restaurant needs its cook. Jess comes to the restaurant. His back hurts. Jess usually sits at the counter. Mr. Brashov tells him to sit on a chair at a table. The chair will be better for his back.

When Rosa arrives at work, she tells everyone about her water problems. Rosa tries to call the landlord, but she gets the answering machine. Jamal offers to help Rosa. He goes to her apartment after work to look at the pipes. The pipes are very old, and there is a leak. The sink needs a new faucet, too.

While Jamal is fixing the pipe under Rosa's sink, he accidentally breaks Rosa's radio. He takes the broken radio with him so he can fix it.

Rosa is very unhappy about the problems in her apartment building. She decides to write a letter to the building manager. Katherine tries to help. She thinks Rosa's letter is too nice. She gives Rosa suggestions to make the letter stronger. Katherine says, "Say the building is dirty. There are rats everywhere." Rosa is not sure Katherine's suggestions are good ideas.

Jess walks in the cafe. He sees Henry with a video camera. Henry tells Jess, "I'm making a documentary for my class. It's about work." Henry's teacher, Michael McAllister, is a reporter for a local TV station. Henry is filming everyone at the café.

A man comes to Crossroads Café. He is looking for Rosa. He is from the property management company for her building. Rosa did not pay her rent because her apartment needs repairs. Rosa says, "I need some repairs done. My bathroom faucet leaks." The man tells Rosa she must pay, so she gives him a check for the rent. Henry has his video camera, and he films Rosa and the man. This makes the man angry.

Katherine wants to help Rosa. She thinks Rosa should fight for changes in her building. Jess tells Rosa to ask the other tenants for help. Mr. Brashov tells Rosa to have a tenants' meeting at Crossroads Café. Everyone will help her. Jamal will make some signs, and Henry and Katherine will help set up the café for the meeting.

Henry brings Michael McAllister to the meeting. The tenants make a list of all the problems in their building. They elect Rosa president of their group. Then a stranger comes in. His name is Dr. Martinez, and he wants to help the tenants.

The next day at the restaurant, Henry turns on the TV and everyone watches the news. They see a story about the meeting at Crossroads Café. They find out about Dr. Martinez. He invested money in Rosa's building, and he is one of the owners. Before the meeting Dr. Martinez didn't know about the problems. Now he wants to help.

Dr. Martinez comes into the restaurant to see Rosa. He invites her to a meeting with his investment partners. They want to discuss the problems in Rosa's apartment building.

Henry gets his grade for the video. It's a B plus. He didn't get a better grade because his video was not about the topic—work.

UNIT 18 OPPORTUNITY KNOCKS

TEACHER'S NOTES AT A GLANCE

	ACTIVITIES	MATERIALS	TIME
CLASS OPENER	◆ discussion		5–10 minutes
YOUR NEW LANGUAGE	*Do before worktext* ◆ replay **Word Play** ◆ brainstorm ◆ discussion ◆ play **Story Clip #1** ◆ card game ◆ comparing music (Ext. Act. #1)	TV/VCR board TV/VCR Handout 18-A music/CD or cassette player, board	2–5 minutes 10–15 minutes 5–10 minutes 5–10 minutes 10–15 minutes 20–30 minutes
IN YOUR COMMUNITY	◆ 3-step interview ◆ discussion & role-play ◆ design business cards (Ext. Act. #2)	board Handout 18-B card stock, colored markers	5–10 minutes 10–20 minutes 20–30 minutes
READ AND WRITE	◆ reading practice ◆ interview	sample cover letters job coach	10–30 minutes 10–20 minutes
WHAT DO YOU THINK?	*Do before worktext* ◆ play **Story Clip #2** ◆ play **Story Clip #3** ◆ problem-solving	TV/VCR TV/VCR Handout 18-C	5–10 minutes 10–15 minutes 10–15 minutes
CULTURE CLIP	*Do before worktext* ◆ replay **Culture Clip** ◆ survey ◆ think-pair-share ◆ interview	TV/VCR board Handout 18-D	2–5 minutes 5 minutes 5–10 minutes 10–15 minutes
EPISODE WRAP UP	◆ discussion	board	5–10 minutes

VIDEO HIGHLIGHTS	
13:06–14:52	**Word Play:** Comparing things
17:51–20:21	**Culture Clip:** Worker safety
1:41–4:40	**Story Clip #1:** Mr. Brashov has a surprise for the employees at Crossroads Café.
4:57–7:54	**Story Clip #2:** Rick Marshall offers his business card to Jamal.
21:31–23:24	**Story Clip #3:** Rick Marshall attempts to bribe Jamal.

See suggestions on page xii in the Introduction.

YOUR NEW LANGUAGE

Replay **Word Play** (13:06–14:52) **before** learners complete this section of the *worktext*. To present the language focus, tell learners you'd like them to compare Jamal's job as a handyman at Crossroads Café with his new job as a compliance engineer at Regal Engineering and Construction.

- Make two columns on the board and label one HANDYMAN and the other ENGINEER.
- Have learners work with partners or in a small group and brainstorm as many things as possible that they know about each job.
- Debrief the pair or group work using **roundrobin** and write the information under the appropriate columns on the board.
- Use the information on the board to model one or two sentences that make comparisons, for example:

   Jamal's salary is higher at the construction company.
   Jamal's hours are longer at Regal Construction than at Crossroads Café.

- Have learners work again with their partners to write as many sentences as they can comparing Jamal's new and old jobs.
- Have each pair or group share one sentence with the class.

If there is time and learners need more practice, have learners compare their own past and present jobs.

Before learners complete **Handout 18-A**, play **Story Clip #1**. Use the *silent viewing* video technique.

STORY CLIP #1
_____

TIME CODES: 1:41–4:40   **COUNTER TIMES:**

SCENE: Mr. Brashov has a surprise for the employees at Crossroads Café.

FIRST LINE: CUSTOMER: Excuse me, can I get some toast with this?

LAST LINE: I don't know who's in a worse mood—Mr. Brashov or Jamal.

- Play the clip several times with the sound off and have learners work with partners to write what they think Jess, Mr. Brashov, Rosa, and Jamal are saying.
- Play the clip again with sound so learners can compare their dialogues to the clip.
- Have learners share their dialogues with the rest of the class.

Conclude by asking learners to talk about the clip using comparison sentences, for example:

   The jukebox will make Crossroads Café busier.
   Jamal is angrier than usual.

Handout 18-A is a card game. Learners make comparisons. First they tell which of two things they prefer. Then they give a reason using a sentence with a word ending in *er* or a sentence using the word ***more***. Write one or two model sentences on the board.

EXAMPLES: Hot dogs are cheap**er** than hamburgers.

Game shows are **more** interesting than situation comedies.

Extension Activity #1 provides learners with opportunities to make comparisons while discussing their favorite music.

- ◆ Ask learners to bring to class cassettes or CDs of their favorite music.
- ◆ While learners talk about the music they have brought to class, make a chart on the board, like the one below.
- ◆ Make a separate column for each type of music.
- ◆ Write the titles of the music in the appropriate columns.
- ◆ Play two songs and have learners compare them, either orally or in writing.

EXAMPLES: The first song is faster than the second song.

I like the first song better.

CLASSICAL	ROCK	COUNTRY	FOLK

IN YOUR COMMUNITY

Before learners do this section of the *worktext* have learners do a ***3-step interview*** about business cards. Use the following questions or make up your own.

Do people ever give you business cards?

What do you do with them? Where do you keep them?

Are business cards popular in your native country?

Who uses business cards in your native country?

Ask learners to bring business cards to class for additional reading and discussion practice. Make overhead transparencies or photocopies of the business cards and have learners ask and answer questions about them.

Handout 18 B is a discussion about business cards and a role-play.

Extension Activity #2 provides learners with an opportunity to design business cards for Crossroads Café employees or themselves.

- ◆ Cut card stock larger than actual business cards so they will be easier to design and read. Hand out blank card stock to learners.
- ◆ Tell learners to design business cards for a Crossroads Café employee or themselves.
- ◆ Display the completed cards for all learners to see.

READ AND WRITE

Writing a good cover letter to accompany a résumé is a difficult task for both native and nonnative speakers of English. For additional practice with cover letters, after learners have completed the *worktext* pages, do one or more of the following:

- Collect as many cover letters as you can for learners to read and discuss with partners or in small groups.
- Give learners a cover letter with a number of grammatical errors. Have them circle the errors and correct them.
- Invite to class a job coach, personnel director, or someone who is responsible for hiring people. Ask learners to interview the guest about what he or she looks for in cover letters and résumés.

WHAT DO YOU THINK?

Before learners complete this section of the *worktext*, **play Story Clip #2**.

STORY CLIP #2

TIME CODES: 4:57–7:54   **COUNTER TIMES:**

SCENE: Rick Marshall is talking on his cellular phone. He watches Jamal; then he gives his business card to Jamal.

FIRST LINE: MARSHALL: I don't care what they say.

LAST LINE: ALL: Yeah . . . good idea. . . .

- Play the clip and ask learners to look for reasons why Rick Marshall was interested.
- Write learners' responses on the board after you play the clip.
- Play the clip again and have learners tell you to stop the video when they see reasons for Rick's interest in Jamal.

   EXAMPLE: Rick Marshall was interested in Jamal because he was rude to the customer who wanted to know when the jukebox was going to be fixed.

Handout 18-C is a problem-solving activity. **Before** learners complete the handout, **play Story Clip #3**—the scene in which Rick Marshall attempts to bribe Jamal. Use the *retelling the story* video technique.

STORY CLIP #3

TIME CODES: 21:31–23:24   **COUNTER TIMES:**

SCENE: After Jamal tells Mr. Marshall about a problem with the support beams, Mr. Marshall attempts to bribe him.

FIRST LINE: RICK MARSHALL: Come in, Jamal.

LAST LINE: JAMAL: Yes . . . I'd like the number of the Department of Building and Safety.

CULTURE CLIP

Replay **Culture Clip** (17:51–20:21) at least twice **before** learners complete this section of the *worktext*. The first time you play the clip, have learners make a list of the special clothing and safety equipment they see. The second time you play the clip, have learners make a list of employment benefits for workers.

Do a hand survey to discover what kinds of safety clothing and equipment learners use at work. Use the questions below or make up your own. Ask learners to raise their hands if their answers are yes.

> *Do you wear safety glasses at work?*
>
> *Do you wear a hard hat at work?*
>
> *Do you wear special shoes at work?*
>
> *Do you wear a back support belt to protect your back at work?*
>
> *Do you wear ear protectors at work?*
>
> *Do you wear a ground strap at work?*

Have learners do a **think-pair-share** about safety at work. Ask them to discuss these questions or make up your own.

> *Do you wear safety equipment at work?*
>
> *Have you ever had an accident at work? What happened?*
>
> *What's dangerous about your job?*
>
> *What can you do about it?*

After learners have completed this section of the *worktext*, have them do **Handout 18-D**, an interview about benefits. Debrief by writing the information on the board.

EPISODE WRAP UP

Before learners complete **Check Your English** have a discussion about the title of this episode, "Opportunity Knocks."

- Draw a door on the board. Then draw a large hand knocking on the door.
- Ask the class what they think the expression "Opportunity Knocks" means.
- Ask learners to share with the class similar expressions from their native languages.
- Write these expressions on the board:

  Look before you leap.
  When one door closes, another opens.

- Have learners discuss in small groups how they think the two expressions above relate to Jamal.
- Debrief using *teams share*.

CARD GAME

HANDOUT 18-A

Mr. Brashov bought a jukebox for Crossroads Café to attract more customers. Which do you prefer? A quiet restaurant or a restaurant with music?

◆ Work with a partner or a small group.
◆ Write two more choices on the blank cards.
◆ Cut the cards on the lines, scramble them, and put them face down in a pile.
◆ One person turns over a card.
◆ The person reads the card aloud, says which thing she prefers and gives a reason.

> EXAMPLE: *I prefer hot dogs. Hot dogs are cheaper than hamburgers.*

Don't forget to use **er** or **more** in your sentences!

✂ -

hot dogs or hamburgers?	game shows or situation comedies?
cooking or cleaning?	country music or rock and roll?
running or walking?	houses or apartments?
new cars or used cars?	escalators or elevators?
cities or suburbs?	glasses or contact lenses?
dogs or cats?	long hair or short hair?
airplanes or trains?	Italian food or Chinese food?

HANDOUT 18-B

When Rick Marshall met Jamal, he gave him a business card. Then he told Jamal to call him. Jamal called, and Mr. Marshall offered him a job.

♦ Work with a partner.
♦ Read the business cards below.
♦ Write a reason why you would call the person on each card.
♦ Select two cards and role-play conversations.
♦ Share one role-play with the class.

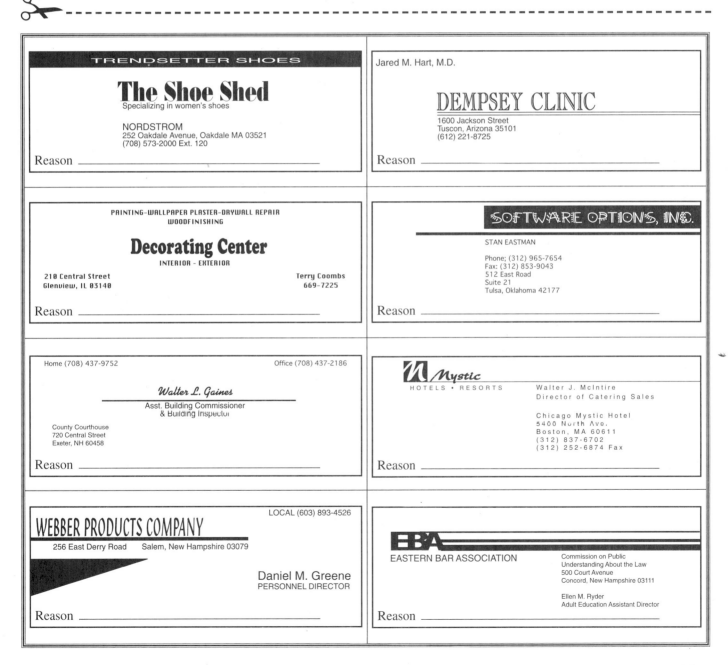

TRENDSETTER SHOES

The Shoe Shed
Specializing in women's shoes

NORDSTROM
252 Oakdale Avenue, Oakdale MA 03521
(708) 573-2000 Ext. 120

Reason _____

Jared M. Hart, M.D.

DEMPSEY CLINIC

1600 Jackson Street
Tuscon, Arizona 35101
(612) 221-8725

Reason _____

PAINTING–WALLPAPER PLASTER–DRYWALL REPAIR
WOODFINISHING

Decorating Center
INTERIOR - EXTERIOR

210 Central Street
Glenview, IL 03140

Terry Coombs
669-7225

Reason _____

SOFTWARE OPTIONS, INC.

STAN EASTMAN

Phone; (312) 965-7654
Fax: (312) 853-9043
512 East Road
Suite 21
Tulsa, Oklahoma 42177

Reason _____

Home (708) 437-9752   Office (708) 437-2186

Walter L. Gaines
Asst. Building Commissioner
& Building Inspector

County Courthouse
720 Central Street
Exeter, NH 60458

Reason _____

Mystic
HOTELS • RESORTS

Walter J. McIntire
Director of Catering Sales

Chicago Mystic Hotel
5400 North Ave.
Boston, MA 60611
(312) 837-6702
(312) 252-6874 Fax

Reason _____

WEBBER PRODUCTS COMPANY

LOCAL (603) 893-4526

256 East Derry Road   Salem, New Hampshire 03079

Daniel M. Greene
PERSONNEL DIRECTOR

Reason _____

EBA
EASTERN BAR ASSOCIATION

Commission on Public
Understanding About the Law
500 Court Avenue
Concord, New Hampshire 03111

Ellen M. Ryder
Adult Education Assistant Director

Reason _____

SOLVE THE PROBLEM

HANDOUT 18-C

Jamal's boss tried to bribe him to sign some papers. But Jamal didn't accept the bribe. He called the Department of Building and Safety; then he quit his job. Do you know people who have had problems like Jamal?

♦ Work with a partner or in a small group.
♦ Read the problem cards.
♦ Write one more problem on the blank card.
♦ Choose one or two problems to discuss.
♦ Make one or two suggestions to solve the problem.
♦ Share the suggestions with the class.

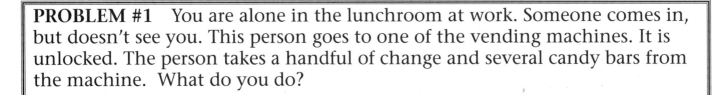

PROBLEM #1   You are alone in the lunchroom at work. Someone comes in, but doesn't see you. This person goes to one of the vending machines. It is unlocked. The person takes a handful of change and several candy bars from the machine. What do you do?
PROBLEM #2   You are shopping at a department store. It's very busy. There is only one clerk, and there are six customers behind you in line. When you get home, you review your bill. The clerk charged you twice for one sale item. She didn't charge you for another item. What do you do?
PROBLEM #3   You have new neighbors, a single father and his three children. The children are 4-, 6-, and 8-years old. You notice the father leaves the children home alone several times a week at night. What do you do?
PROBLEM #4   Your house is for sale. The real estate agent asks if there are any problems with the house. Should you tell the real estate agent the roof leaks? You didn't fix the roof, but you painted the ceiling so the water marks don't show. What do you do?
PROBLEM # 5

HANDOUT 18-D

Most paychecks show employees' benefits.

♦ Read the paycheck below.

♦ Work with a partner and answer the questions.

♦ Write your answers on the lines.

Builders Barn	Builders Barn, Inc. 712 Main Street San Antonio, Texas 78228			CHECK NO: 328537 CHECK DATE: 10/27/96 PERIOD ENDING: 10/22/96 PAY FREQUENCY: BIWEEKLY			
Marcelo Sala 1453 South St. Allenvale, IL 60139	SSN: 332-00-5807 EXEMPTIONS: FED: 00 TAX ADJ: FED:	STATE: 00 STATE:	NUMBER: 0332645807 STATE CODE: PRI: IL SEC: SDI/UC ALT:	TAX STATUS: SINGLE LOCAL CODE: LOC1: LOCAL ALT: BASE RATE: 7.9000	LOC2:	LOC3:	

HOURS AND EARNINGS					TAXES AND DEDUCTIONS			SPECIAL INFORMATION
DESCRIPTION	CURRENT HOURS/UNITS	EARNINGS	Y-T-D HOURS/UNITS	EARNINGS	DESCRIPTION	CURRENT AMOUNT	Y-T-D AMOUNT	
REGULAR	64.00	505.60			SO SEC TAX	39.18	673.71	
VACATION	8.00	63.20			MEDICARE TAX	9.16	157.56	
BIRTHDAY	8.00	63.20			FED INC TAX	79.80	1314.89	
					PRI-STATE TAX	18.96	325.94	
TOTAL H/E	80.00	832.00			TOTAL TAXES	147.10	2472.10	
PRE-TAX ITEMS					AFTER-TAX DEDUCTIONS			
					CASH		202.96	
					EMPLOYEE CLUB		21.00	
TOTAL PRE-TAX								
TOTAL	80.00	632.00			TOTAL PER DED		223.96	

GROSS		PRE-TAX	TAXABLE WAGES	LESS TAXES	LESS DED	EQ NET PAY	
CURRENT	632.00	.00	632.00	147.10	.00	484.90	
Y-T-D	10866.32	.00	10866.32	2472.10	223.96	8170.26	

1. What is Marcelo's gross salary? _____

2. How much does he pay to Social Security? _____

3. How much does he pay for health insurance? _____

4. How many sick days does he have? _____

5. How many vacation days does he have? _____

6. Are there any other deductions for benefits? What are they? _____

_____

Write one or two more questions to ask a partner about this paycheck.

♦ Interview each other about job benefits in your native countries.

♦ Write your partner's answers on the spaces below.

♦ Share the information with the class.

INTERVIEW	NAME:	NATIVE COUNTRY:
1. Do paychecks have deductions for government-funded pensions?		
2. Do paychecks have deductions for health insurance?		
3. Do paychecks show vacation and sick days?		
4. What other benefits are on paychecks?		
5. What other deductions are on paychecks?		

UNIT 18 OPPORTUNITY KNOCKS

Mr. Brashov is looking out the window. Jess asks, "Who are you looking for?" Mr. Brashov says, "Not who, what." Jess then says, "What?" But Mr. Brashov won't tell him. It's a surprise.

Jamal is trying to fix a toaster. He is very unhappy. When Mr. Brashov asks about the toaster, Jamal gets angry.

Mr. Brashov's surprise comes. It's a jukebox. Now Crossroads Café be Crossroads Musical Café! People like to listen to music. Music will bring more customers to Crossroads Café.

Mr. Brashov plugs in the jukebox. Nothing happens. No music. He calls for Jamal. He wants Jamal to fix the jukebox. But Jamal is still angry.

A customer is talking on a cellular phone. He is watching Jamal. He hears Jamal say, "I'm an engineer, not a jukebox engineer." When another customer asks Jamal about the jukebox, Jamal is rude to him. Before the customer with the cellular phone leaves, he gives Jamal his business card. The man's name is Rick Marshall. He owns a construction company. He tells Jamal to call him.

Jamal visits Rick Marshall, and he offers Jamal a job. Mr. Marshall needs a compliance engineer for his company. A compliance engineer makes sure the construction work matches the building plans. Jamal accepts the job.

At the café, Mr. Brashov wants Jamal to make a sign for the café about the jukebox. But Jamal quits his job at Crossroads Café.

Jamal is at the construction company. Mr. Marshall shows Jamal around the job site and introduces him to other employees. Joe Cassidy, a project manager, gives Mr. Marshall an envelope.

Jamal is alone in the construction office at night. The phone rings. He goes to Mr. Marshall's desk to answer the phone. It's Jihan. While Jamal is talking to his wife, he spills some coffee. It falls on an envelope with computer disks.

Jamal is worried about the disks. He wipes the coffee off the disks. Then he puts a disk in the computer to check it for damage. Jamal sees something on the disk. It's a crack in one of the beams for a building at the construction site.

At the café, Mr. Brashov decides to put two ads in the newspaper—one ad is for a handyman and the other ad is for the jukebox. He wants to sell it. The jukebox is too much trouble!

Jamal talks to Mr. Marshall. He wants Jamal to sign some papers. Jamal doesn't want to sign them. He knows the building is not safe. Mr. Marshall gives Jamal an envelope with many one hundred dollar bills in it. It's a bribe to get Jamal to sign the papers. After Mr. Marshall leaves the office, Jamal picks up the telephone. He calls the Department of Building and Safety.

Mr. Brashov is interviewing applicants for the handyman job. He is having no luck finding a new handyman. Then Jamal walks in. He says, "I heard you are looking for a handyman. I'm here to apply for the job."

Jamal is working for Crossroads Café again—not Crossroads Musical Café. Mr. Brashov sold the jukebox.

UNIT 19 — THE PEOPLE'S CHOICE

TEACHER'S NOTES AT A GLANCE

	ACTIVITIES	MATERIALS	TIME
CLASS OPENER	♦ discussion		5–10 minutes
YOUR NEW LANGUAGE	*Do before worktext* ♦ replay **Word Play** ♦ think-pair-share ♦ categorizing ♦ role-play	TV/VCR board board Handout 19-A	3–5 minutes 5–10 minutes 5–10 minutes 10–15 minutes
IN YOUR COMMUNITY	♦ roundrobin ♦ interview ♦ reading practice (Ext. Act. #1) ♦ make a budget (Ext. Act. #2) ♦ survey	board photocopies overhead transparencies, tax/utility bills board Handout 19-B	10–15 minutes 15–30 minutes 15–20 minutes 15–25 minutes 15–20 minutes
READ AND WRITE	♦ play **Story Clip #1** ♦ 3-step interview	TV/VCR, Handout 19-C board	10–15 minutes 15–20 minutes
WHAT DO YOU THINK?	♦ play **Story Clips #2 & 3** ♦ prepare a speech ♦ reading & listening practice (Ext. Act. #3)	TV/VCR newspapers; radio; TV	5–10 minutes 30–45 minutes 10–20 minutes
CULTURE CLIP	♦ replay **Culture Clip** ♦ discussion	TV/VCR Handout 19-D	2–5 minutes 10–20 minutes
EPISODE WRAP UP	♦ discussion ♦ sides activity	board	5–10 minutes 5–10 minutes

VIDEO HIGHLIGHTS	
17:36–19:07	**Word Play:** Making promises
9:44–12:10	**Culture Clip:** Local government
3:15–5:54	**Story Clip #1:** Jess decides to run for city council.
6:13–8:04	**Story Clip #2:** Jess makes his first speech.
19:15–21:05	**Story Clip #3:** Jess makes his last speech.

CLASS OPENER

See suggestions on page xii of the Introduction.

YOUR NEW LANGUAGE

Replay **Word Play** (17:36–19:07) **before** learners complete this section of the *worktext*. To introduce the language focus do a ***think-pair-share*** about promises. Write the questions below on the board or make up your own. Before you begin, however, remind learners they do not have to reveal anything they feel is too personal. The discussion is about promises, not secrets!

Think about a promise you made recently. What happened?
Think about a promise someone made to you recently. What happened?
Think about a promise you broke. How did you feel?
Think about a promise someone else broke. How did you feel?

Debrief the pairs in a whole class discussion. As the pairs share, write their responses on the board. Then have the class categorize them. Some suggestions for categories are: people, promises to change, promises to do something, and feelings about the promises.

A variation is to have learners discuss promises made by elected officials, both in the United States and in learners' native countries. Ask what kinds of promises were made, which were kept, and why some were broken.

Handout 19-A is a card game and role-play.

IN YOUR COMMUNITY

Invite a local elected official to visit your class. To prepare learners for the visit, do a ***roundrobin*** of questions they'd like to ask. Then,

- Make copies of the questions.
- Give one copy to the elected official who will be interviewed.
- Give the other copies to the learners.
- Have each learner choose a question to ask.
- Have learners check off each question as it is asked at the interview.
- Encourage additional questions if there is time.

As a follow-up to the visit, have learners write thank-you notes.

Extension Activity #1 provides additional reading practice and discussion. Ask someone who lives in the community for a copy of their real estate tax bill. Then do the following:

- Cover or white-out personal information on the bill.
- Make an overhead transparency of the bill. Then make photocopies to distribute to the class.
- Have learners scan the bill to find the answers to questions you ask about the taxes detailed on the bill.

    EXAMPLES: *How much are the taxes for the elementary schools?*
    How much are the taxes for the community college?

- Debrief by circling the answers on the overhead transparency of the tax bill.

A variation is to bring in additional utility bills (garbage, cable TV, electric, telephone, or gas) for reading practice.

Extension Activity #2 provides practice making a budget and comparing expenses. Begin by doing a survey about budgets. Ask learners to raise their hands if their answer is yes. Ask,

Do you think you spend too much money?
Do you have money to cover emergencies?
Do you make a family budget?
Do you stick to the budget?
Do you think the federal government spends too much money?
Do you think your local government spends too much money?

To introduce the group activity:

- Ask, *What happened when Jess called to complain about his water bill?* (He was told to pay the bill, and then he'd get a refund.)
- Ask, *Would you pay an incorrect bill and wait for a refund?*

Then do the following:

- Divide learners into mixed-ability groups.
- Have each group brainstorm a list of monthly expenses (rent, car payment, water bill, and so on.)
- Have each group select one person to take the list to another group. That group checks to see if they have other suggestions.
- Have each group look over the suggestions and decide whether or not to add them to its list.
- Give each group a monthly income. The group makes a budget to cover expenses.
- Post the budgets and give learners time to look at each one.

Handout 19-B is a survey about learners' satisfaction with their communities. While you debrief the learners' responses, make a chart on the board like the following one.

NAME OF COMMUNITY	NAME OF COMMUNITY	NAME OF COMMUNITY
Housing		
Transportation, etc.		
(write in the categories that were rated and their scores)		

- Have learners discuss which community has the highest satisfaction ratings.
- To review the making comparisons activity, have learners use the information in the chart.

READ AND WRITE

Mr. Brashov has spent two weeks trying to talk to someone about the construction traffic in front of Crossroads Café. Jess complains about a $30,000 water bill to his friends at the café and ends up running for city council because he has a complaint about his water bill.

Play **Story Clip #1** while learners complete **Handout 19-C.**

STORY CLIP #1

TIME CODES: 3:15–5:54   **COUNTER TIMES:**

SCENE: It's late morning when Jess enters the café.

FIRST LINE: MR. BRASHOV: Ah, good morning, Jess.

LAST LINE: JESS: The people's choice. I like the way that sounds.

- ◆ **After** learners have checked the order of their dialogue cards, play the clip again.
- ◆ While learners are watching the clip, have them work with a partner to make a list of all of the reasons why Jess decides to run for city council.
- ◆ Replay the clip as many times as necessary.
- ◆ Debrief by writing the learners' responses on the board.
- ◆ End by asking, *Have you ever felt the way Jess does?*

Before learners write a letter of complaint about a utility bill, have a class discussion about the complaints learners have had. If there are any learners who have not had complaints, the discussion will give them some ideas. To begin the discussion,

- ◆ write the words MONTHLY and BIMONTHLY on the board.
- ◆ point to the word MONTHLY. Ask learners to name the utilities they pay monthly and write the utilties on the board.
- ◆ do the same for BIMONTHLY. (In some states, gas bills are bimonthly during the summer months. Water and garbage bills are frequently bimonthly as well.)
- ◆ Ask learners to think about any complaints they've had about monthly bills. Write the complaints on the board.
- ◆ do the same for BIMONTHLY.
- ◆ have learners do a *3-step-interview* about problems they have had with utility bills and what happened.
- ◆ debrief using **stand up and share.**

▶ WHAT DO YOU THINK?

Before learners complete the *worktext* pages for this section, play **Story Clips #2** and **#3** and use the *thinking and feeling* video technique for both clips. **Story Clip #2** shows Jess's first speech, an impromptu one, at Crossroads Café. **Story Clip #3** shows Jess's last speech. Have learners compare Jess's first speech to his last speech.

STORY CLIP #2

TIME CODES: 6:13–8:04   **COUNTER TIMES:**

SCENE: It's lunchtime at Crossroads Café. Jess is reading the results of a voter survey in the newspaper.

FIRST LINE: JAMAL: Hassan, it's still crooked.

LAST LINE: CUSTOMER #3: Can I have the check?

```
┌─────────────────────────────────────────────────────────────────┐
│  STORY CLIP #3                                                    │
│                                                                   │
│  TIME CODES:  19:15–21:05          COUNTER TIMES:                 │
│                                                                   │
│  SCENE:  Crossroads Café is open for a campaign rally for Jess.   │
│                                                                   │
│  FIRST LINE:  DAN MILLER:  OK, Mr. Councilman. Knock'em dead.     │
│                                                                   │
│  LAST LINE:  JESS:  I'll make only one promise, and that is to    │
│              work for the interests of the people in this         │
│              community. Thank you very much.                      │
└─────────────────────────────────────────────────────────────────┘
```

After learners have compared Jess's two speeches, survey the learners about their experiences making speeches. Ask learners to raise their hands if their answer is yes. Ask,

> *Did you take public speaking in school?*
> *Have you ever made a speech?*
> *Have you ever wanted to make a speech?*
> *Do you want to learn how to make a speech?*

If learners raise their hands for the last question, and if you have time, have learners prepare and give 1–3 minute speeches about a topic related to **What Do You Think?** or any other topic they are interested in.

Extension Activity #3 provides learners with opportunities to read and discuss political campaigns. In the United States, elections are generally held in the fall and spring, but aspiring candidates campaign all year long. If learners are interested, have them bring news stories about political candidates (local, state, and national) to class. Photocopy the stories and use them for reading practice.

You also might want to tape radio or TV news stories related to politics for authentic listening practice.

▶ CULTURE CLIP

Replay **Culture Clip** (9:44–12:10) **before** learners complete this section of the worktext.

Before learners complete **Handout 19-D**, find out how many, if any, are thinking about becoming U.S. citizens. If a substantial number are preparing for the citizenship exam, you might want to expand **Handout 19-D** to include more information.

▶ EPISODE WRAP UP

Before learners complete **Check Your English**, have a discussion about the title of this episode, "The People's Choice."

- ♦ Write the title on the board.
- ♦ Ask learners why, at the beginning of the episode, Jess called himself "the People's Choice"?
- ♦ Ask learners if Jess was "the People's Choice" when he let Dan Miller and Andrew Comstock advise him?
- ♦ Ask learners why Jess really was "the People's Choice," at the end of the video, even though he lost the election.

End with a *sides* activity. Have learners go to one side of the room if they would have voted for Jess, and to the other side if they wouldn't have voted for him. Have learners share their reasons with the class.

ROLE-PLAY

HANDOUT 19-A

Jess told voters, "I promise you I'll be the best councilman this city has ever had." What other promises do the people in the story make?

♦ Work with a partner or in a small group.
♦ Cut the cards on the lines.
♦ Write more names on the blank cards.
♦ Scramble the cards and put them face down in a pile.
♦ Take turns. One person turns over a card and makes a promise. The other person asks questions about the promise.
♦ Share one or two promises with the class.

✂ -

Jess to Carol	Mr. Brashov to Jess
Carol to Jess	Dan Miller to Jess
Andrew Comstock to Jess	Henry to Mr. Brashov
Rosa to Katherine	Jamal to Mr. Brashov

INTERVIEW

HANDOUT 19-B

Jess and Mr. Brashov had complaints about their city. Jess got a $30,000 water bill. Mr. Brashov called the city to complain about construction traffic. Are there problems in your community?

- ◆ Interview a partner.
- ◆ Ask questions about his or her community.
- ◆ Circle the numbers in the chart and write comments on the lines.
- ◆ Share the information with a small group.
- ◆ Report the groups' information to the class.

NAME: _____ COMMUNITY: _____

INTERVIEWER: _____

How satisfied are you with your community? Circle the numbers. Tell how you feel and explain why.

	Very Satisfied	Satisfied	Dissatisfied	Very Dissatisfied
Housing	1	2	3	4
Transportation	1	2	3	4
Cleanliness	1	2	3	4
Police Protection	1	2	3	4
Schools	1	2	3	4
Library	1	2	3	4
Taxes	1	2	3	4
Parks	1	2	3	4

Other:

Overall rating:

Comments: _____

_____

_____

_____

DIALOGUE

HANDOUT 19-C

Jess complains about his water bill. His friends at Crossroads Café tell him to run for city council. His wife, Carol, also thinks it's a good idea.

- ◆ Work with a partner.
- ◆ Read the dialogue cards below.
- ◆ While you watch the video, put the conversation in order.
- ◆ Share with another pair. Is the order of the cards the same?

✂ -

MR. BRASHOV: What's this?
MR. BRASHOV: Thirty thousand dollars for one month of water?
KATHERINE: What a city.
MR. BRASHOV: Sure. How about Mayor Brashov?
HENRY: Or Councilman Washington.
JAMAL: Yes, but you were a manager with the post office.
HENRY: We could all help.
JESS: I'm telling you, Carol, I've had it up to here with this city.
CAROL: You know this city like the back of your hand.
JESS: The people's choice. I like the way that sounds.

WHAT DO YOU KNOW?

HANDOUT 19-D

Jess decided to run for city council.

- ♦ Ask your classmates the questions below.
- ♦ Write their answers in the chart below.
- ♦ Ask each classmate only one question.
- ♦ Share the answers with the class.

QUESTION	ANSWER
1. Who is the president of the United States?	
2. Who is the vice president?	
3. When is Election Day?	
4. How many senators are there in the United States?	
5. How many representatives are there?	
6. Who are the senators in your state?	
7. Who is your representative?	
8. Who is the governor of your state?	
9. What is the state capitol?	
10. Who is the mayor of your city?	
11. What is the legal voting age in the United States?	
12. What is the national anthem?	
13. Have you ever campaigned for anyone? Who?	
14. Have you ever met a politician? Who?	
15. Have you ever run for a political office?	

UNIT 19 THE PEOPLE'S CHOICE

Mr. Brashov is unhappy. There is construction in front of Crossroads Café, and it is keeping customers away. Mr. Brashov calls the city office to complain, but he can't find anyone to speak to.

A young Middle Eastern man enters the café. He tells Mr. Brashov, "People are putting pieces of wood on the street in front of your café." Mr. Brashov doesn't know the man, but he looks familiar.

Jamal enters. He asks, "Has anyone seen my cousin?" The young Middle Eastern man enters the café again. He's Jamal's cousin Hassan. Jamal introduces him to everyone. Hassan likes Rosa very much. Hassan is in the United States to learn English. He wants to be a tour guide in Egypt.

Later that morning, Jess comes to the café. He shows his water bill to Mr. Brashov. Jess's bill for one month of water is $30,000. Jess called the city to complain, but nobody helped him.

Both Jess and Mr. Brashov are unhappy with the city. Mr. Brashov tells Jess to run for city council.

Later at home, Jess talks to his wife, Carol, about Mr. Brashov's idea. Carol thinks it's a good idea, too. She says to Jess, "You could be the *people's choice.*"

Jess decides to run for city council. Crossroads Café becomes his campaign headquarters. There are posters and flyers in the café for Jess Washington, the "People's Choice." But nobody knows Jess, and his name is not mentioned in the newspaper polls.

Mr. Brashov has an idea. He wants Jess to make speeches at Crossroads Café while people are eating. Only one customer is interested in Jess's first speech. His name is Dan Miller.

Dan Miller tells his boss, Mr. Comstock, about Jess. Andrew Comstock is a businessman. He wants to help elect someone to the city council. If Andrew Comstock helps Jess, Jess will help him. Dan brings Mr. Comstock to the café to see Jess.

Dan Miller and Mr. Comstock have a lot of ideas to help Jess. They change his looks, and they give him ideas for speeches. One day, Jess is sitting at a table in Crossroads Café, and nobody recognizes him. Jess is wearing a toupee!

Carol is not happy with the new Jess. She will not vote for him. She doesn't like Mr. Comstock either. He thinks more about money than people.

Jess is giving another speech at Crossroads Café. When Jess sees Carol, he changes his speech. He takes off his toupee. He is the old Jess, and Mr. Comstock is very angry. He won't help Jess anymore.

Hassan is getting ready to return to Egypt. He tries to give Rosa a goat. This is a marriage proposal custom in Egypt. Rosa is very surprised. She likes Hassan, but she doesn't want to marry him.

Election night arrives. Everyone is at Crossroads Café. They are waiting to hear the election results. The phone rings, and Katherine answers it. Jess has 18,706 votes and Tom Johansen has 19,706 votes. Jess didn't win the election, but he didn't lose either.

UNIT  OUTSIDE LOOKING IN

TEACHER'S NOTES AT A GLANCE

	ACTIVITIES	MATERIALS	TIME
CLASS OPENER	◆ discussion		5–10 minutes
YOUR NEW LANGUAGE	*Do before worktext* ◆ replay **Word Play** ◆ think-pair-share ◆ roundrobin ◆ play **Story Clip #1** ◆ giving advice ◆ conversation practice (Ext. Act. #1)	TV/VCR board TV/VCR Handout 20-A board	3–5 minutes 10–15 minutes 10–15 minutes 3–5 minutes 15–20 minutes 10–15 minutes

IN YOUR COMMUNITY	*Do before worktext*
	◆ survey
	◆ 3-step interview
	◆ information gap
	◆ Venn Diagram
	  (Ext. Act. #2)
	◆ design movie rating
	  system (Ext. Act. #3)
		
		board
		Handout 20-B
		board, paper
		
		paper, markers
			
			5–10 minutes
			10–15 minutes
			10–15 minutes
			15–20 minutes
			
			20–30 minutes

READ AND WRITE	*Do before worktext* ◆ play **Story Clip #2** ◆ discussion	 TV/VCR, paper	 3–5 minutes 5–10 minutes
WHAT DO YOU THINK?	◆ sides *Do after worktext* ◆ play **Story Clip #3**	 TV/VCR	0–20 minutes 5–10 minutes
CULTURE CLIP	*Do before worktext* ◆ replay **Culture Clip** ◆ problem-solving ◆ interview	 TV/VCR, paper Handout 20-C Handout 20-D	 3–5 minutes 15–20 minutes 15–30 minutes
EPISODE WRAP UP	◆ discussion ◆ think-pair-share ◆ journal writing	board	5 minutes 10 minutes 5–15 minutes

VIDEO HIGHLIGHTS	
12:08–13:35	**Word Play:** Giving advice
16:23–19:30	**Culture Clip:** Raising children
3:25–5:33	**Story Clip #1:** Andrew Collins asks Rosa for a favor.
21:41–24:11	**Story Clip #2:** Rosa goes to Andrew's apartment and finds him packing.
24:38–25:39	**Story Clip #3:** Bill returns from his convention in Chicago.

CLASS OPENER

See suggestions on page xii of the Introduction.

YOUR NEW LANGUAGE

Replay **Word Play** (12:08–13:35) **before** learners complete this section of the *worktext*. Introduce the language focus.

- ♦ Tell learners you are planning to visit their countries. Have learners work in same-country groups to make lists of advice about what you should do there. Debrief using *teams share.*
- ♦ Ask learners to do a *think-pair-share* about the last time they gave advice to someone. Who were they talking to? What advice did they give?
- ♦ Do a *roundrobin* and write learners' responses on the board.

Play **Story Clip #1**. Andrew Collins has come to Crossroads Café to ask Rosa for a favor.

STORY CLIP #1

TIME CODES: 3:25–5:33   **COUNTER TIMES:**

SCENE: Andrew Collins asks Rosa for a favor.

FIRST LINE: JESS: So how's it going back there, Victor?

LAST LINE: ANDREW: See you tonight.

- ♦ **While** learners are watching the story clip, ask them to make a list of advice for Rosa to follow as a translator for Andrew.
- ♦ **After** the clip, have learners share their lists with their partners.
- ♦ Debrief in a large group discussion.

If there is time, have learners role-play Crossroads Café characters giving advice to Rosa.
Handout 20-A provides learners with additional practice giving advice. Debrief by asking each group of learners to share some of its advice with the rest of the class.
Extension Activity #1 provides conversation practice.

- ♦ Ask learners what Katherine and Andrew collect (stuffed animals and art).
- ♦ Write the characters' names, JAMAL, ROSA, JESS, HENRY, and VICTOR, on the board.
- ♦ Have learners work with partners or in small groups to brainstorm ideas about what the characters might or should collect based on what the learners know about the characters.
- ♦ Debrief using *teams share* and *best idea.*
- ♦ End the discussion by asking learners to share with the class what, if anything, they collect.
- ♦ Ask for volunteers to bring in examples of their collections to class.

IN YOUR COMMUNITY

Before learners complete this section of the *worktext,* do a hand survey about movies. Use the following questions or make up your own. Ask learners to raise their hands if their answer is yes. Ask,

Do you watch movies in English on TV?
Do you watch movies in your native language on TV?
Do you rent movies from a video store?
Do you go to a movie theater to see movies?

Do you go to a movie theater <u>once a week</u>? (Substitute other time expressions such as once a month or once or twice a year for the underlined words.)

Do you like to watch <u>comedies</u>? (Substitute these words for the underlined words: dramas, action adventure, science fiction, romance, etc.)

Follow the survey with a *3-step interview* about the movies learners have seen recently. Write these questions on the board.

What is the name of the last movie you saw?

Where did you see it?

Who were the actors?

What kind of movie was it? What was the rating?

Would you recommend this movie? Why or why not?

Did you read, listen to, or watch a review about this movie before you saw it?

Handout 20-B is an *information gap*. Learners ask and answer questions about movie listings. Debrief by making a class chart of movies the learners have seen recently, where they saw them, what time of day they went to the movies, and how much they paid.

Extension Activity #2 provides additional conversation practice about the topic of movies. Learners compare and contrast going to movie theaters in the United States to movie theaters in their native countries.

♦ Draw a large **Venn Diagram** on the board.

♦ Have learners copy the diagram on their papers.

♦ Divide learners into same-ethnicity groups if possible.

♦ Ask learners to think about these questions:

How is going to the movies the same in your country as in the United States?

How is going to the movies different in your country from the United States?

♦ Have each group complete a **Venn Diagram**. In the circles on the left and right, learners write differences between movie theaters in their countries and the United States; where the circles intersect, learners write similarities.

♦ Post the **Venn Diagrams** and give learners time to look at them and ask questions.

Extension Activity #3 provides learners with an opportunity to discuss and design their own movie rating systems.

♦ Call learners' attention to the explanation of movie ratings in the worktext.

♦ Have learners work in mixed ability pairs or groups.

♦ Distribute paper and markers.

♦ Ask learners to design their own rating systems for movies.

♦ Give learners time to share their rating systems with the class.

READ AND WRITE

Play **Story Clip #2 before** learners complete this section of the *worktext*. Use *behavior study* and *role-play* video techniques. In this story clip, Rosa goes to Andrew's apartment and finds him packing.

STORY CLIP #2

TIME CODES: 21:41–24:11   **COUNTER TIMES:**

SCENE: Rosa goes to Andrew's apartment and finds him packing.

FIRST LINE: ROSA: Hi, Andrew. I got here as soon as I could.

LAST LINE: ROSA: And by the way, I hate goose liver!

♦ Have learners draw a chart like the following one on their papers.

ROSA	ANDREW	LIBBY	MAID

♦ While learners watch the clip, have them write words about each character's behavior in the appropriate column, e.g., what they are doing, what they are saying.
♦ Debrief in a large class discussion.
♦ Ask learners to think about how the clip would have been different if Andrew and Libby had apologized to Rosa.
♦ Ask for volunteers to role-play Libby and Andrew apologizing to Rosa.
♦ Have learners write an apology from Andrew or Libby to Rosa and share it with a partner, group, or the class.

WHAT DO YOU THINK?

Before learners complete this section of the *worktext,* do a *sides activity*. Ask some of the following questions or make up your own. Debrief each question before you ask the next one.

Is Andrew Collins a jerk?
Do you like Rosa with blond hair ?
Do you think Rosa will do any more translating jobs?
Do you think Henry and Jamal really changed Stuart?
Do you think Mr. Shuster will give Mr. Brashov a break on his rent?
Do you think Bill's proposal was romantic?
Do you think Katherine should marry Bill?
Do you think Katherine's children will be happy about Bill?

Play **Story Clip #3 after** learners have completed the exercises in the worktext. Use the *thinking and feeling* and *freeze-frame* video techniques.

STORY CLIP #3

TIME CODES: 24:38–25:39   **COUNTER TIMES:**

SCENE: Bill returns from his convention in Chicago.

FIRST LINE: MR. BRASHOV: Hello, Bill.

LAST LINE: KATHERINE: Yes!

Bill pays another surprise visit to Crossroads Café. He brings two presents for Katherine—a stuffed bear and an engagement ring.

♦ Pause the video at the following scenes, and ask learners to describe what the characters are thinking and feeling, when . . .
   Katherine starts to open her present.
   Katherine picks up the second box.
   Bill puts the ring on Katherine's finger.
   Katherine says, "Yes."

♦ Make a chart like the following one on the board. As you debrief learners about what Katherine and Bill are thinking, fill in the chart.

	THINKING	FEELING
Katherine		
Bill		

If there is time, end the discussion by asking learners to share stories about how their spouses or parents proposed marriage.

CULTURE CLIP

Replay **Culture Clip** (16:23–19:30) **before** learners complete the exercises in the *worktext*. **While** learners watch the clip, have them make a list of the general topics that are discussed in the clip (the importance of having children, lack of rules, respect for elders, lack of understanding about culture, mothers staying at home, material things, and television). Replay the clip as many times as needed.

♦ Divide learners into mixed-ability groups.
♦ Have learners compare and contrast what the people in the clip said with their own opinions about the topics mentioned.
♦ Debrief using *teams share*.

Handout 20-C is a problem-solving activity. Learners discuss parenting problems and offer solutions.

Handout 20-D is an interview. Learners compare child-rearing in the United States with child-rearing in their native countries.

EPISODE WRAP UP

Discuss the title of this episode, "Outside Looking In."

♦ Write the title on the board.
♦ Ask, "Who was outside looking in?"
♦ Have learners do a *think-pair-share* about the reasons why Rosa was an outsider.
♦ Encourage learners to write in their journals about times when they were outsiders.

GIVE ADVICE

HANDOUT 20-A

People use *should* to give advice to their friends, families, neighbors, and coworkers. People use *had better* for strong advice or warnings.

- ◆ Work with a partner or in a small group.
- ◆ Cut out the cards, scramble them, and put them face down in a pile.
- ◆ One person turns over a card and reads it aloud.
- ◆ The other people in the group, give advice about the topic or person on the card—orally or in writing.

EXAMPLE: HENRY—TABLES
Henry should clean the tables as soon as the customers leave.

✂ -

HENRY—TABLES	KATHERINE—BILL	MR. SHUSTER—RENT
JAMAL—BABYSITTER	BILL—BEAR	STUART—PLAY
MR. BRASHOV—ORDER SUPPLIES	ANDREW—ROSA	RICARDO—ENGLISH
ROSA—HAIR	LIBBY—ROSA	ROSA-MAID

INFORMATION GAP

HANDOUT 20-B

PARTNER A

Rosa and Katherine want to go to the movies. What time should they go and what should they see?

♦ Work with a partner.
♦ Ask and answer questions about the movie schedules below.
   EXAMPLE: A: *How much are the movies at Glendale Square?*
            B: *$1.00*
♦ Write the missing information in the blanks.
♦ Together agree on a movie and time.

GLENDALE SQUARE _____ All Shows 847-921-8564	WESTGATE $1.00 til 6 P.M. $1.75 after 6 P.M.	NORTH AVENUE
Tall Women _____ 1:30, 4:45, 7:20	**Cold** (R) _____ only	**Tall Women** _____ 2:00, 4:15, 7:00
Helicopter (PG-13) _____, 9:50	**Going to L.A.** _____ 2:15, _____, 7:00	**The Journey** (R) 2:00, 4:00, _____, 9:00
Going to L.A. (R) 1:20, 5:10, _____	**Peaches** (PG) _____, 7:20, 9:30	**Falling Asleep** (R) 5:15, 7:10, 9:10

PARTNER B

Rosa and Katherine want to go to the movies. What time should they go and what should they see?

♦ Work with a partner.
♦ Ask and answer questions about the movie schedules below.
   EXAMPLE: B: *What are the times for Tall Women?*
            A: *1:30, 4:45, and 7:20.*
♦ Write the missing information in the blanks.
♦ Together agree on a movie and time.

GLENDALE SQUARE $1.00 All Shows 847-921-8564	WESTGATE til 6 P.M. $1.75 after 6 P.M.	NORTH AVENUE $2
Tall Women (R) 1:30, _____, 7:20	**Cold** _____ 7:30 only	**Tall Women** (R) 2:00, 4:15, _____
Helicopter _____ 7:30, _____	**Going to L.A.** (R) _____, 4:40, 7:00	**The Journey** (R) 2:00, 4:00, 7:00, 9:00
Going to L.A. (R) _____, 5:10, 7:40	**Peaches** (PG) 3:15, 7:20, _____	**Falling Asleep** _____ 5:15, _____, 9:10

Teacher's Resource Book B ===== **69**

SOLVE THE PROBLEM

HANDOUT 20-C

Mr. Shuster worries about his son, Stuart. He acts like an adult, not a child. It is hard work to raise a child.

♦ Work with a partner or in a small group.
♦ Read and discuss the problems below.
♦ Write one more problem on the blank card.
♦ Give the problem to another pair or group to discuss.
♦ Share your suggestions with the class.

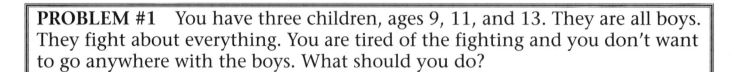

PROBLEM #1   You have three children, ages 9, 11, and 13. They are all boys. They fight about everything. You are tired of the fighting and you don't want to go anywhere with the boys. What should you do?

PROBLEM #2   Your daughter is 13-years old. You do not like her friends. When they come to your house, they never even say hello. Your daughter is not doing her homework, and she lies to you about everything. You also think she is stealing from your wallet. What should you do?

PROBLEM #3   Your daughter is 16-years old. She got her driver's license one month ago. So far, she has had one accident and one ticket for speeding. The cost of your car insurance is going up. You are worried. What should you do?

PROBLEM #4   You have a 3-year old boy. He is afraid of everything. He wants the lights on when he sleeps and he wants you to sleep with him. He doesn't want to play outside because he is afraid of spiders, bees, and dogs. When dogs bark, he cries. He follows you everywhere, and he wants you to hold him all of the time. You are tired and worried. What should you do?

PROBLEM # 5

INTERVIEW

HANDOUT 20-D

How are ideas about raising children in your native country different from ideas in the United States?

♦ Interview a partner about parenting.
♦ Ask the questions below and put checkmarks in the correct columns.
♦ Write four more questions and ask them, too.
♦ Share the answers with the class.

	IN MY COUNTRY		IN THE UNITED STATES	
	YES	NO	YES	NO
1. Do people usually have more than two children?				
2. Do parents want boys more than girls?				
3. Do parents hire babysitters for their children?				
4. Do children go to preschool?				
5. Do children have a lot of expensive toys?				
6. Do children have chores to do at home?				
7. Do children get money for doing chores at home?				
8. Do children have a lot of time to play with other children?				
9.				
10.				
11.				
12.				

It's Monday morning. Rosa and Katherine are talking about the weekend. Rosa begins to tell Katherine about a guest teacher. But she is interrupted.

Bill comes to say good-bye to Katherine. He is going to a conference in Chicago. Katherine reminds Bill, "Don't forget my bear." Katherine collects stuffed animals.

Mr. Brashov asks Rosa about lunch. He wants to have a special dessert with lunch because Mr. Shuster, his landlord, is coming to talk about a new lease.

Mr. Shuster tells Mr. Brashov, "You have a wonderful restaurant." Then he gives Mr. Brashov some bad news. The taxes have gone up, and he will probably have to increase the rent.

A man comes into the café. Rosa recognizes him. It's her guest teacher, Andrew Collins. Rosa is very nervous when she talks to Andrew Collins. She tells him about the lunch special. But Mr. Collins doesn't want lunch. He wants to ask Rosa for a favor. Mr. Collins needs a translator for a meeting at his home. Rosa agrees to help him.

Mr. Shuster finishes lunch. Mr. Brashov is nervous about the new lease. He wants to meet with Mr. Shuster and his accountant. But Mr. Shuster is very busy. His son, Stuart, is coming home from school next week. Mr. Shuster's son has to write a school paper about how to run a small business. When Mr. Brashov hears this, he offers to help Stuart.

Rosa is at Andrew Collins' apartment. The furniture is very expensive, and there are a lot of antiques and artwork. One guest, Libby Flanders, is rude to Rosa. She asks Rosa her opinion about a painting. Then she tells Rosa, "You do not belong here."

A few days later at work, Rosa is studying. She's trying to learn about art, music, and wine so she can talk to Andrew and his friends.

Mr. Shuster brings Stuart to Crossroads Café. Mr. Brashov is very surprised. Stuart looks like an 11- or 12-year old. But he dresses and talks like an adult.

Rosa is at Andrew's apartment again. Now she has blond hair, and she talks about art and wine. Andrew is surprised.

At the café, Stuart makes Jamal angry. Jamal and Henry take Stuart out of the café. This worries Mr. Brashov. He calls after them, "You aren't going to do anything violent, are you?"

When Jamal and Henry bring Stuart back to the café, he looks different. His hair is uncombed, and he is dirty. He was playing soccer with Henry and Jamal. Then Mr. Shuster comes in. He's happy about the way Stuart looks. Stuart looks like a kid!

Rosa goes to Andrew's apartment. Andrew is going to Switzerland. Rosa is very disappointed. She enjoyed her dates with Andrew, but they were not dates to him. They were business.

Back at the café, there is one more surprise. Bill is back from Chicago. He kisses Katherine and gives her a big box. Inside, there are two presents, a stuffed bear and an engagement ring.

UNIT 21 WALLS AND BRIDGES

TEACHER'S NOTES AT A GLANCE

	ACTIVITIES	MATERIALS	TIME
CLASS OPENER	♦ discussion		5–10 minutes
YOUR NEW LANGUAGE	*Do before worktext* ♦ replay **Word Play** ♦ discussion *Do after worktext* ♦ play **Story Clip #1** ♦ language practice ♦ conversation practice (Ext. Act. #1)	TV/VCR board TV/VCR Handout 21-A	2–5 minutes 10–15 minutes 5–10 minutes 10–15 minutes 10–15 minutes
IN YOUR COMMUNITY	*Do after worktext* ♦ play **Story Clip #2** ♦ scanning practice ♦ discussion and role-play	TV/VCR report cards Handout 21-B	5–10 minutes 15–30 minutes 15–25 minutes
READ AND WRITE	*Do after worktext* ♦ discussion ♦ cultural awareness (Ext. Act. #2)	 thank-you cards, stationery	10–15 minutes 15–25 minutes
WHAT DO YOU THINK?	*Do after worktext* ♦ listening practice	TV/VCR, Handout 21-C	10–15 minutes
CULTURE CLIP	*Do before worktext* ♦ replay **Culture Clip** ♦ interview ♦ unscramble sentences & sequence ♦ memory game (Ext. Act. #3)	TV/VCR photocopy questions Handout 21-D 10–15 objects, tray	2–5 minutes 20–30 minutes 15–20 minutes 15–20 minutes
EPISODE WRAP UP	♦ dictation ♦ discussion ♦ journal writing	paper board	10–20 minutes 5–10 minutes 5–15 minutes

VIDEO HIGHLIGHTS	
10:31–12:16	**Word Play:** Asking for and offering help
18:55–22:16	**Culture Clip:** Becoming a citizen
3:35–4:52	**Story Clip #1:** Chris Scanlon asks Rosa for help.
12:19–14:22	**Story Clip #2:** Rosa and Chris Scanlon go to Mr. Hernandez's tailor shop.
22:48–25:31	**Story Clip #3:** Mr. Brashov and Mr. Hernandez talk about their daughters.

CLASS OPENER

See suggestions on page xii of the Introduction.

YOUR NEW LANGUAGE

Replay **Word Play** (10:31–12:16) **before** learners complete this section of the *worktext*. Introduce the language focus.

- Draw two columns on the board.
- Write ASKING FOR HELP at the top of one column and OFFERING HELP at the top of the other column.
- Ask learners to think about the last time they requested help and write their responses in the first column.
- Ask learners to think about the last time they offered to help someone and write their responses in the second column.
- Discuss the request and offers.

After learners have completed the pages in the *worktext,* play **Story Clip #1.** Use the *retelling the story* video technique.

STORY CLIP #1
_____

TIME CODES: 3:35–4:52   **COUNTER TIMES:**

SCENE: Chris Scanlon asks Rosa for help.

FIRST LINE: KATHERINE: Hi. Sit anyplace you'd like.

LAST LINE: CHRIS: Thank you.

Handout 21-A provides learners with practice asking for and offering help. Debrief by having each pair or group share one role-play with the class.

Extension Activity #1 provides additional conversation practice.

- Divide learners into mixed-ability groups.
- Ask learners to make lists of all of the offers and requests for help in this video episode.
- Debrief using *teams share*.

IN YOUR COMMUNITY

After learners have completed this section of the *worktext,* play **Story Clip #2** and use the *watchers and listeners* video technique.

TIME CODES: 12:19–14:22   **COUNTER TIMES:**

SCENE: Rosa and Chris Scanlon go to Mr. Hernandez's tailor shop.

FIRST LINE: CÉSAR: Is this about the skirts?

LAST LINE: MARÍA: I'm sorry.

♦ Write the following questions on the board or make up your own.

Who went to talk to Mr. Hernandez?
What did they want to talk about?
How did Mr. Hernandez react?
Why did Mr. Hernandez pretend not to speak English?
How did María react?
What will happen next?

♦ Have a class discussion about how learners felt when their teachers talked to their parents about their report cards or other school-related problems.

Collect a variety of report cards and transcripts (different grades and schools including community colleges and universities) for additional reading and discussion practice.

♦ Make overhead transparencies and photocopies of the report cards, grade reports, or transcripts.
♦ Distribute the photocopies to mixed-ability groups.
♦ Have learners scan the photocopies for specific information and answer questions similar to the ones about María's report card in the *worktext*.
♦ Encourage learners to ask questions about anything they don't understand on the photocopies.
♦ End by having learners compare report cards, grade reports, or transcripts in the United States to their native countries.

Handout 21-B is a discussion and role play activity. Explain to learners that they need not be parents to contribute good ideas!

READ AND WRITE

After learners have completed the exercises in the *worktext*, have a discussion about what other kinds of thank-you notes characters in this episode might write.

Extension Activity #2 is a cultural awareness activity. The variety and abundance of cards may be overwhelming for many language learners. The following activity may assist them in making appropriate purchases.

♦ Bring a variety of commercial thank-you notes to class.
♦ Number each example and display it on a table.

- Ask learners to number a piece of paper according to the number of samples you have.
- Hold up each example and ask:

    Would you send this card to anyone?
    Who would you send it to?
    Why would you send it?

- Have learners share their answers with partners or in small groups.

WHAT DO YOU THINK?

Handout 21-C provides active listening practice. Play **Story Clip #3 while** learners put the dialogue cards in order.

STORY CLIP #3

TIME CODES: 22:48–25:31   **COUNTER TIMES:**

SCENE: Mr. Brashov and Mr. Hernandez talk about their daughters.

FIRST LINE: MR. BRASHOV: I did it! I am going to be a citizen!

LAST LINE: CÉSAR: Tomorrow we will talk to Mrs. Scanlon.

After learners have completed **Handout 21-C**, have them do a *3-step interview* about what made César Hernandez change his mind about the work-study program. Debrief using *best idea only*.

A variation is to write learners' ideas on the board and have learners vote for the reason they think best explains César's change of mind. Possible reasons are:

- César was worried he'd become estranged from his daughter as Victor did.
- Victor reminded César why he came to the United States.
- César realized he was treating María differently than he would a son.
- María tells César she is not ashamed that he is a tailor.

CULTURE CLIP

Replay Culture Clip (18:55–22:16) before learners complete this section of the *worktext*. Invite one or more newly naturalized citizens to class to be interviewed or to be part of a panel discussion.

- Before the guests arrive, have learners brainstorm a list of questions to ask.
- Make photocopies of the questions and distribute copies to the learners and the guests (so they know what to expect).
- Have learners practice asking the questions before the guests arrive.
- Encourage learners to write thank-you notes to the guests.

Handout 21-D is a scrambled word and sequencing activity about the steps to naturalization.

Extension Activity #3 is a memory game. Mr. Brashov had difficulty studying for his citizenship test because he couldn't remember what he read.

- Ask learners to raise their hands if they have good memories.
- Tell learners they can demonstrate how good their memories are by playing this simple game.
- Put 10–15 different objects on a tray.
- Ask for a volunteer to look at the objects for 1 minute.
- Take away the tray and ask the learner to name as many of the objects as he or she can.
- Do this several times.
- Ask the volunteers to share their strategies for remembering the objects.
- Have the rest of the class share additional strategies.

A variation is to have learners read a list of 20 words, one word at a time, take the list away, and then ask learners to recall the first six words, the last six words, words that appeared more than once, words that caught their attention, etc.

The memory check helps learners see **how** they remember, not how much they remember. Usually learners who categorize, visualize, or use word associations remember more words than those who do not. The memory check also helps learners who have limited strategies for remembering learn about other strategies.

EPISODE WRAP UP

Before learners discuss the title of this episode, do the following dictation activity.

The dictation part of the citizenship test is often very difficult, and applicants applying for naturalization often benefit from extensive practice. Dictate the following sentences which retell the subplot of this video episode.

> *Mr. Brashov was studying for his citizenship test.*
> *His friends offered to help him study, but he refused their help.*
> *The night before the test, he changed his mind.*
> *Jess and Katherine helped him study.*
> *Mr. Brashov passed the test.*

For additional dictation practice, have learners take turns dictating sentences to each other about the main plot.

Have a discussion about the title of this episode, "Walls and Bridges."

- Write the title on the board.
- Ask learners to explain what walls are.
- Ask learners what the walls were for Mr. Brashov, Mrs. Scanlon, Mr. Hernandez, and María.
- Ask learners to explain what bridges are.
- Ask learners what the bridges were for each of the characters.
- Encourage learners to write in their journals about some walls and bridges in their lives.

ROLE-PLAY

HANDOUT 21-A

Jess offered to help Mr. Brashov study several times. Finally Mr. Brashov accepted Jess's help—the night before his citizenship test.

- ◆ Work with a partner or in a small group.
- ◆ Cut the cards, scramble them, and put them face down in a pile.
- ◆ Person **A** turns over a card and reads it aloud to Person **B**. They follow the directions on the card.

EXAMPLE:

> *OPEN CAR DOOR*
> A: *offer help*
> B: *say no*

A: *Would you like me to open the car door?*
B: *No, thanks. I can do it myself.*

 -

TURN OFF THE COMPUTER	ANSWER THE PHONE	GIVE A CUSTOMER A MENU
A: ask for help B: say yes	A: offer help B: say no	A: ask for help B: say yes
PIN UP THIS HEM	MAKE A FOOD DELIVERY	WATCH THE KIDS AFTER SCHOOL
A: ask for help B: say no	A: offer help B: say yes	A: ask for help B: say yes
TAKE A PICTURE	LOCK THE FRONT DOOR	PUT THE CLOSED SIGN IN THE WINDOW
A: offer help B: say no	A: ask for help B: say yes	A: ask for help B: say no
FIX THE CHAIR	FILL OUT THE WORK-STUDY FORM	OPEN THE DOOR
A: offer help B: say yes	A: ask for help B: say yes	A: ask for help B: say no

ROLE-PLAY

HANDOUT 21-B

María stopped going to school because she had to work in her family's tailoring shop. Mrs. Scanlon, one of her teachers, tried to help María.

♦ Work with a partner or in a small group.
♦ Read the problems below.
♦ For each problem, write suggestions for parents and teachers on the lines.
♦ Write one more problem and give it to another pair or group to write suggestions.
♦ Role-play one of the problems for the class.

#1 Cecilio is in kindergarten. He hits the other children and yells at them. He has no friends.		#2 Jin is in 4th grade. He doesn't like math. He doesn't know his multiplication tables.	
PARENTS	**TEACHER**	**PARENTS**	**TEACHER**
_____	_____	_____	_____
_____	_____	_____	_____
_____	_____	_____	_____
_____	_____	_____	_____
_____	_____	_____	_____

#3 Larissa is in 8th grade. She was an A student. Now she gets Cs and Ds, and she doesn't want to go to school.		#4 _____ _____ _____	
PARENTS	**TEACHER**	**PARENTS**	**TEACHER**
_____	_____	_____	_____
_____	_____	_____	_____
_____	_____	_____	_____
_____	_____	_____	_____
_____	_____	_____	_____

DIALOGUE

HANDOUT 21-C

Mr. Brashov and Mr. Hernandez talk about citizenship and their daughters. Why does Mr. Hernandez change his mind about the work-study program?

♦ Work with a partner.
♦ Read the dialogue cards below.
♦ While you watch **Story Clip #3**, put the conversation in order.
♦ Share with another pair. Is the order of the cards the same?

✂ --

MR. BRASHOV: César, stay a minute.
CÉSAR: Congratulations. You must be very proud.
MR. BRASHOV: We don't speak, we don't visit.
MR. BRASHOV: You still have your daughter with you.
MR. BRASHOV: Would you insist that he quit school?
MR. BRASHOV: But this is America.
CÉSAR: You think I should allow this work-study?
CÉSAR: Is being a tailor so terrible?
MARÍA: I love you, Papa, and I respect you.
CÉSAR: Tomorrow, we will talk to Mrs. Scanlon.

UNSCRAMBLE AND SEQUENCE

HANDOUT 21-D

Mr. Brashov wants to become a U.S. citizen. Here are the steps.

♦ Work with a partner or in a small group.
♦ Cut the cards.
♦ Put the scrambled words into sentences.
♦ Add capital letters and periods.
♦ Put the sentences into order according to what Mr. Brashov said first, second, third, and so on.
♦ Share your sentences with another group.

✂ -

have	three	photographer	take	a
color	yourself	of	photos	

your	get	fingerprints	taken
police	a	at	station

get	from	citizenship	application	a
and	Naturalization	the	Immigration	Service

the	out	fill	form	and	with
it	send	$95.00	to	INS	

interview	for	the	prepare	and
study	for	test	citizenship	the

interview	to	the	report
with	documents	supporting	your

and	the	United	civics
history	take	States	test

test	the	interview	and	pass	and
the	to	go	ceremony	in	swearing

UNIT 21 WALLS AND BRIDGES

Crossroads Café is closed. Mr. Brashov and Rosa are planning menus for the week. María Hernandez comes into the café. She is bringing dinner to her father, César. César is the evening janitor at Crossroads Café. César is also a tailor, and he owns a tailoring shop in the neighborhood.

María shows a photo to Rosa. It is from Big Sister Week at María's school. Rosa is María's "Big Sister," and Rosa is very proud of María. She won a science award at school.

The next day, Mr. Brashov and Jess are playing chess. Jess asks Mr. Brashov about his citizenship exam. Mr. Brashov is studying, but it is very hard. Jess offers to help Mr. Brashov study. But Mr. Brashov refuses Jess's help.

María's teacher, Chris Scanlon comes in the café. She is looking for Rosa. Chris is worried about María because she isn't coming to school anymore. Chris doesn't speak Spanish so she asks Rosa to talk to María's parents.

Rosa goes to the Hernandez's tailoring shop. César is pinning the hem of Rosa's skirt. María is surprised to see Rosa. Rosa tells María about Mrs. Scanlon's visit. María is uncomfortable. Her father doesn't want her to talk to Rosa.

Finally, Rosa asks César, "Why isn't María in school?" César needs María to work in his shop. Rosa is very angry when she hears César's reasons. She wants to do something to help María.

María comes to Crossroads Café to say hello to Rosa. Henry tells María about the work-study program. Students go to school for half a day and work for half a day. Rosa thinks this would be a good way for María to continue school.

Rosa and Mrs. Scanlon go to the tailoring shop. They want to tell Mr. Hernandez about the work-study program. He is not interested. María will get married and have children. She does not need an education.

Mr. Brashov's citizenship test is tomorrow. He can't remember anything. Jess and Katherine offer to help him study. Mr. Brashov finally accepts their help. He also asks Jess to go with him to the interview.

The next day, Mr. Brashov is very excited. He passed the citizenship test. Everyone congratulates him.

Mr. Hernandez comes into the café. Mr. Brashov tells him the news about his citizenship test. Mr. Brashov is very happy, but he is also a little sad. Mr. Brashov's daughter doesn't know about her father's good news. They had a fight, and they don't speak to each other. Mr. Hernandez thinks about Mr. Brashov's problems with his daughter. Mr. Brashov talks about his daughter to Mr. Hernandez.

María comes in the café. She brings her father's dinner. César asks María, "Is it terrible to be a tailor?" María says, "No Papa, not for you." But María doesn't want to be a tailor. She wants to do other things. She wants an education.

Mr. Hernandez surprises María. He finally agrees to talk to Mrs. Scanlon about the work-study program. María can go back to school.

UNIT 22 HELPING HANDS

TEACHER'S NOTES AT A GLANCE

	ACTIVITIES	MATERIALS	TIME
CLASS OPENER	◆ discussion		5–10 minutes
YOUR NEW LANGUAGE	*Do before worktext* ◆ replay **Word Play** ◆ *think-pair-share* ◆ language practice ◆ conversation practice (Ext. Act. #1)	TV/VCR board Handout 22-A	2–5 minutes 10–15 minutes 15–20 minutes 5–10 minutes
IN YOUR COMMUNITY	*Do after worktext* ◆ brainstorming/ categorizing ◆ conversation and reading practice (Ext. Act. #2) ◆ play **Story Clip #1**	board résumé ads TV/VCR, Handout 22-B	10 minutes 20–30 minutes 10–15 minutes
READ AND WRITE	*Do before worktext* ◆ play **Story Clip #2**	TV/VCR, board	10–15 minutes
WHAT DO YOU THINK?	*Do after worktext* ◆ play **Story Clip #3** ◆ interview	TV/VCR, board Handout 22-C	10–15 minutes 15–20 minutes
CULTURE CLIP	*Do before worktext* ◆ replay **Culture Clip** ◆ list making/ discussion ◆ matching ◆ interview or panel discussion	TV/VCR paper Handout 22-D	2–5 minutes 5–10 minutes 10–15 minutes 30–45 minutes
EPISODE WRAP UP	◆ discussion	board	5–10 minutes

VIDEO HIGHLIGHTS	
15:52–17:37	**Word Play:** Asking for and giving permission
7:10–9:57	**Culture Clip:** Financial difficulties
21:21–24:11	**Story Clip #1:** The employees at Crossroads Café help Frank get ready for a job interview.
10:01–12:40	**Story Clip #2:** Jamal arrives at the hotel.
18:30–20:17	**Story Clip #3:** Jamal and Jihan have an argument.

CLASS OPENER

See suggestions on page xii of the Introduction.

YOUR NEW LANGUAGE

Replay **Word Play** (15:52–17:37) **before** learners complete this section of the *worktext*. Introduce the language focus.

♦ Make a chart like the following one on the board.

WHAT	WHO	ANSWER	WHERE

♦ Write these questions on the board:

What did you ask permission to do?
Who did you ask? Did the person say yes or no?
Where were you?

♦ Have learners do a ***think-pair-share*** about asking for permission.
♦ Debrief using ***roundrobin*** and write learners' responses in the chart on the board.

After learners have completed the pages in the *worktext,* have them complete **Handout 22-A.** Ask each pair to choose one conversation to share with the class. **Extension Activity #1** provides additional conversation practice.

♦ Divide learners into mixed-ability groups.
♦ Ask learners to think about the video and make a list of as many requests for permission as they can remember.
   Example: Frank said, "Do you mind if I take a look at the circuit box?"
♦ Debrief using ***teams share***.

IN YOUR COMMUNITY

After learners have completed this section of the *worktext,* have a discussion about résumés.

♦ Have the class brainstorm a list of as many jobs as they can think of.
♦ Write the jobs on the board.
♦ Have learners work with partners to sort the jobs into two categories: jobs that require résumés and jobs that don't.
♦ Do a survey about résumés. Ask learners to raise their hands if their answers are yes. Ask:

Did you need a résumé for your current job?
Do you have a résumé?
Do you think you might need a résumé in the future?
Are you interested in writing a résumé?

♦ If learners are interested, invite a job developer, job coach, or employer to class to talk about résumé writing.

Extension Activity #2 provides additional conversation and reading practice on the topic of résumés.

- Collect 3–5 advertisements for résumé-writing services from newspapers or magazines.
- Make photocopies of the ads.
- Divide learners into same-ability groups and give each group one or more ads, depending on the group's ability.
- Have the groups write 3–5 factual questions about each ad.

    EXAMPLES: *What's the name of the résumé service?*
    What's the telephone number?
    How much does a consultation cost?

- Collect the ads and questions then redistribute them to the groups. This time, the groups answer factual questions about the ads.
- Conclude activity with a class discussion about which ad learners think they would call if they need a résumé.
- Ask for several volunteers to call résumé writing services for information about costs, time it takes to have a résumé written, etc. Ask volunteers to report their findings to the class.

Handout 22-B provides sequencing practice.

STORY CLIP #1

TIME CODES: 21:21–24:11   **COUNTER TIMES:**

SCENE: Frank gets ready for his interview with Marty.

FIRST LINE: No dialogue. Scene begins in utility room with Jess and Mr. Brashov doing a mock interview with Frank.

LAST LINE: KATHERINE: You guessed it.

While learners watch **Story Clip #1**, they put events from the clip in order. A variation is to provide learners with 5–7 blank cards and have them write events on the cards while they watch the story clip. Ask learners to exchange cards with their partners or within their small groups; then have learners sequence the cards.

▶ READ AND WRITE

Before learners complete this section of the worktext, **play Story Clip #2** and use the *thinking and feeling* and *silent viewing* video techniques.

STORY CLIP #2

TIME CODES: 10:01–12:40   **COUNTER TIMES:**

SCENE: Jamal has just entered the hotel room and the phone is ringing.

FIRST LINE: JAMAL: Hello . . . hello?

LAST LINE: JIHAN: It's a very busy day tomorrow.

◆ Write these questions on the board.

What was Jamal thinking when he entered the empty hotel room?
How did Jamal feel when he talked to the airline about his lost luggage?
How did Jamal feel when he was trying to talk on the phone and Azza was crying?
How did Jamal feel when he saw Jihan?
What was Jamal thinking when Jihan said she couldn't have breakfast with him?
How did Jihan feel when she couldn't have breakfast with Jamal?

◆ Have learners discuss the questions with their partners. Debrief using **teams share**.

WHAT DO YOU THINK?

After learners complete this section of the *worktext,* **play Story Clip #3** and use the ***behavior study*** video technique.

STORY CLIP #3

TIME CODES: 18:30–20:17   **COUNTER TIMES:**

SCENE: Jamal and Jihan return to the hotel after a party.

FIRST LINE: BABYSITTER: She's been quiet all evening, no trouble at all.

LAST LINE: JAMAL: I don't know what I want.

In this clip, Jihan and Jamal have an argument. Have learners do a *3-step interview.* Write the following questions on the board.

Why is Jamal angry with Jihan?
How does Jihan feel about bringing Jamal and Azza on her business trip?
Why does Jamal feel Jihan puts her job first?
Who is right—Jamal or Jihan?

Handout 22-C is an interview. Learners give their opinions about sentences from the video episode.

CULTURE CLIP

Replay **Culture Clip** (7:10–9:57) **before** learners complete this section of the *worktext.* **While** learners are watching the clip, have them make a list of the financial pressures the people in the clip talk about and the solutions, if any, to the pressures. **After** the clip, discuss the lists and ask learners if there are any things they'd add to the lists.

Handout 22-D is a matching activity. **After** the activity, have a class discussion about the organizations. Ask learners to talk about other helping organizations they know. If there is time, have a class discussion about "helping hands" in learners' native countries.

Extension Activity #3 is an interview or panel discussion. If learners are interested, invite one or more people who are involved in helping organizations to class for a panel discussion or interview by the class. Have the class write questions to ask before the guests come. As a follow up, have the class write thank-you notes.

A variation is to collect short articles or announcements from the newspaper about helping organizations and use them for reading and discussion.

▶ EPISODE WRAP UP

Discuss the title of this episode, "Helping Hands."

- ♦ Write the title on the board.
- ♦ Ask learners, "Who were the helping hands in this episode?"
- ♦ Write the names of the characters on the board.
- ♦ Have learners tell how each person was a helping hand.
- ♦ Encourage learners to write in their journals about one of these: how they would have treated Frank; a situation in which they have been a helping hand; or a situation in which they have received a helping hand.

CARD GAME

HANDOUT 22-A

With a partner, practice asking for permission.

- ◆ Cut the cards and scramble them. Put them face down in a pile.
- ◆ One person turns over a card and shows it to the partner.
- ◆ The first person starts the conversation.
- ◆ The second person turns over the next card and starts the conversation.
- ◆ Share one conversation with the rest of the class.

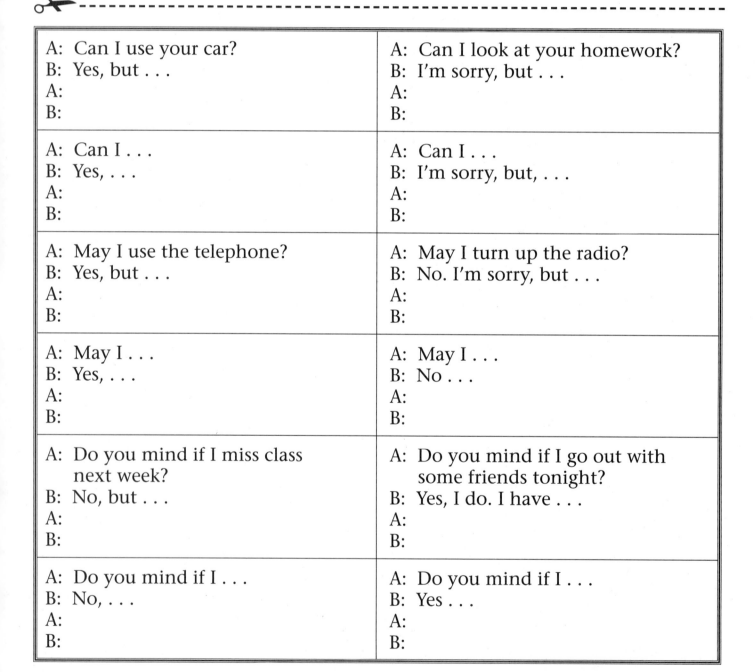

A: Can I use your car? B: Yes, but . . . A: B:	A: Can I look at your homework? B: I'm sorry, but . . . A: B:
A: Can I . . . B: Yes, . . . A: B:	A: Can I . . . B: I'm sorry, but, . . . A: B:
A: May I use the telephone? B: Yes, but . . . A: B:	A: May I turn up the radio? B: No. I'm sorry, but . . . A: B:
A: May I . . . B: Yes, . . . A: B:	A: May I . . . B: No . . . A: B:

A: Do you mind if I miss class
   next week?
B: No, but . . .
A:
B:
	A: Do you mind if I go out with
	   some friends tonight?
	B: Yes, I do. I have . . .
	A:
	B:

A: Do you mind if I . . . B: No, . . . A: B:	A: Do you mind if I . . . B: Yes . . . A: B:

▶ PUT IT IN ORDER

HANDOUT 22-B

Frank hasn't had a job for 18 months. Mr. Brashov, Jess, Katherine, Henry, and Rosa help him get ready for his job interview.

- ◆ Work with a partner.
- ◆ Cut the cards and scramble them. Put them face up.
- ◆ Put the cards in order while you watch the video clip.
- ◆ Share the order of the cards with another pair.
- ◆ Is the order of the cards the same? Discuss any differences.

✂ -

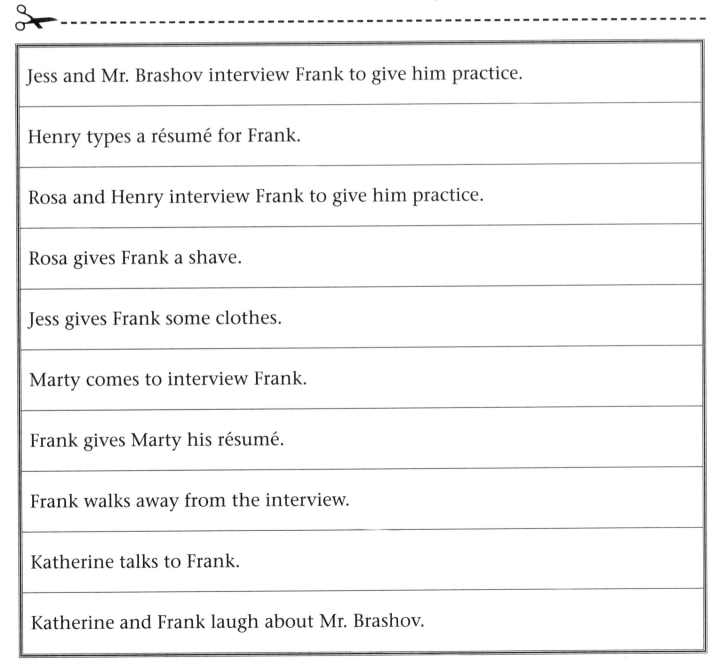

Jess and Mr. Brashov interview Frank to give him practice.

Henry types a résumé for Frank.

Rosa and Henry interview Frank to give him practice.

Rosa gives Frank a shave.

Jess gives Frank some clothes.

Marty comes to interview Frank.

Frank gives Marty his résumé.

Frank walks away from the interview.

Katherine talks to Frank.

Katherine and Frank laugh about Mr. Brashov.

INTERVIEW

HANDOUT 22-C

At first, Katherine didn't like Frank. She didn't want to help him. Then she changed her mind.

- ♦ Read the sentences below.
- ♦ Put checks in the opinion columns.
- ♦ Write two more sentences about the video.
- ♦ Work with a partner.
- ♦ Share your opinions.
- ♦ Did you change any of your opinions after you discussed them? Which ones?

OPINIONS

	AGREE	DON'T KNOW	DISAGREE
1. Mr. Brashov has a kind heart.			
2. Katherine is afraid of Frank.			
3. Frank wants Jamal's job.			
4. Jamal is jealous of his wife's job.			
5. Jamal will never go on another business trip with Jihan.			
6. Jamal should have left Azza at home with a babysitter.			
7. Frank won't keep his new job for long.			
8. Anyone can find a job.			
9.			
10.			

MATCH UP

HANDOUT 22-D

There are many ways to help people. Match the "helping hands" with their descriptions.

- ◆ Work with a partner or a small group.
- ◆ Cut the cards and scramble them. Put them face down.
- ◆ Take turns. Turn over two cards and read them aloud.
- ◆ If the cards match, keep the cards.
- ◆ If the cards don't match, put them face down again. The next person takes a turn.
- ◆ Continue playing until all of the cards are matched.

✂ -

Dial-A-Ride	provides transportation for elderly or disabled people
Habitat for Humanity	builds low-cost housing
Public Action to Deliver Shelter	gives homeless people a place to sleep and food to eat
Mothers Against Drunk Driving	educates people about the dangers of drinking and driving
Meals for Seniors	delivers hot meals to the homes of elderly people
Alcoholics Anonymous	helps people stop drinking
Literacy Volunteers	teaches people to read and write English
Red Cross	provides food, clothing, and medical care during and after emergencies and disasters
United Way	raises money for other helping organizations
Adult Day Care	takes care of elderly people during the day

A man is sitting on a bench outside Crossroads Café. He is reading the newspaper. The man needs to shave, and his clothes are dirty.

Henry looks out the window and sees the man. Katherine says, "He's been out there since this morning. Should we do something?" Jess says, "No. He's just reading the paper."

Mr. Brashov is reading a list from Jamal. Jamal is going on vacation so he is leaving some instructions for Mr. Brashov. Jamal and his daughter, Azza, will meet Jihan on a business trip.

Katherine looks out the window again and sees the man on the bench. She asks, "Mr. Brashov, have you noticed that man sitting out front?" She asks Rosa about the man, too. Only Katherine is worried about the man.

Finally, Katherine opens the door for Jess. The man is at the door. His hands are in his pockets. Katherine asks the man, "What do you want?" He says, "I need something to eat." The man comes into the café. Katherine thinks the man is a robber with a gun. She tells Rosa to make a turkey sandwich for him, quickly.

The man is very nervous. He starts to take his hands out of his pockets. Everyone puts their hands in the air. The man is very confused. He is not a robber. He is just hungry.

The lights go out in the café. The man helps Mr. Brashov fix the lights. Then he introduces himself. His name is Frank. He has not worked for 18 months. Mr. Brashov and Jess want to help him. Katherine does not. She doesn't trust Frank.

The next day at the café, Mr. Brashov is trying to fix a lock. Then Frank comes in and offers to help. Mr. Brashov asks Frank to fill in for Jamal. Frank is the new handyman for a week.

Jess is having car problems. Frank offers to look at Jess's car. Frank used to be a mechanic. When Jess tries to pay Frank, Frank refuses the money.

Jess wants to help Frank. Jess used to work at the post office. He knows about a job there, so he sets up a job interview for Frank.

Frank has good job skills, but he doesn't do well on job interviews. Jess and Mr. Brashov help Frank get ready for the interview. They pretend to interview him. Henry types his resumé. Rosa gives him a shave, and Jess gives him some clothes. Finally, Frank is ready for his job interview.

Jess's friend, Marty, comes to Crossroads Café to interview Frank. Frank is very nervous. He gives Marty his resumé. They talk for a little bit, but then Frank gets up and walks away.

Frank feels very bad. He disappointed Jess and Mr. Brashov. Katherine talks to Frank. She tells him, "I know how you feel. When I came to Crossroads Café, I was very nervous, too."

Katherine gives Frank some advice. She tells him to imagine the interviewer is in his underwear. Then Frank won't be so nervous.

Frank gets another chance to interview with Marty. This time he follows Katherine's advice, and he gets the job!

 UNIT **23** THE GIFT

TEACHER'S NOTES
AT A GLANCE

	ACTIVITIES	MATERIALS	TIME
CLASS OPENER	◆ discussion		5–10 minutes
YOUR NEW LANGUAGE	*Do before worktext* ◆ replay **Word Play** ◆ 3-step interview ◆ play **Story Clip #1** ◆ role-play ◆ roundrobin (Ext. Act. #1)	TV/VCR, board board TV/VCR Handout 23-A, board	2–5 minutes 10–15 minutes 5–10 minutes 15–25 minutes 10–15 minutes
IN YOUR COMMUNITY	*Do before worktext* ◆ survey ◆ discussion ◆ discussion and reading practice ◆ discussion (Ext. Act. #2)	travel brochures, mail-in coupons, travel ads, Handout 23-B state map	5–10 minutes 15–25 minutes 15–25 minutes 10–15 minutes
READ AND WRITE	*Do after worktext* ◆ think-pair share ◆ play **Story Clip #2**	board TV/VCR, board	15–20 minutes 10–15 minutes
WHAT DO YOU THINK?	*Do after worktext* ◆ play **Story Clip #3** ◆ problem-solving	TV/VCR, board Handout 23-C	15–20 minutes 10–15 minutes 15–25 minutes
CULTURE CLIP	*Do before worktext* ◆ replay **Culture Clip** ◆ discussion ◆ interview	TV/VCR Handout 23-D	5–10 minutes 15–10 minutes 15–20 minutes
EPISODE WRAP UP	◆ discussion	board	5–10 minutes

VIDEO HIGHLIGHTS	
16:46–18:19	**Word Play:** Making invitations
10:48–12:47	**Culture Clip:** Taxes
5:55–8:34	**Story Clip #1:** Joe gives Mr. Brashov the keys to his son's cabin.
22:58–25:06	**Story Clip #2:** Mr. Brashov finally celebrates his birthday.
19:41–21:36	**Story Clip #3:** Mr. Brashov goes to the airport to see his daughter.

CLASS OPENER

See suggestions on page xii of the Introduction.

YOUR NEW LANGUAGE

Replay **Word Play** (16:46–18:19) **before** learners complete this section of the *worktext*. Introduce the language focus.

♦ Have learners do a *3-step interview* about making invitations.

♦ Ask learners to think about the last time someone invited them to do something.

Who made the invitation?
What was the invitation?
What happened?

♦ Ask learners to think about the last time they invited someone to do something.

Who did they make the invitation to?
What was the invitation?
What happened?

♦ Debrief the class and write their answers in a chart on the board like the one below.

WHO	INVITATION	ACCEPT	DECLINE

Play Story Clip #1 twice.

STORY CLIP #1

TIME CODES: 5:55–8:34   **COUNTER TIMES:**

SCENE: Joe gives Mr. Brashov the keys to his son's cabin.

FIRST LINE: KATHERINE: I think the answer to our problem just walked in the door.

LAST LINE: MR. BRASHOV: I'll be back in a little while.

First ask learners to listen to the language Joe uses to invite Mr. Brashov to his cabin. (Joe holds up a set of keys and tells Mr. Brashov it's his ticket to paradise.) **After** you play the clip, have learners tell you what Joe said. Ask learners if this is more formal or less formal than the examples in the *worktext*.

Then write these questions on the board and play the clip a second time. **While** learners watch the clip again, have them find the answers to the questions. **After** the clip, have learners discuss their answers with their partners.

Why is Joe the answer to Katherine's problem?
What did Joe give Mr. Brashov?

How far away is the cabin?
What does Katherine give Mr. Brashov?
Where does Mr. Brashov go?

Handout 23-A is a *role-play*. Learners practice making , accepting, and declining invitations using the language in the *worktext* and in the story clip.

Extension Activity #1 provides additional discussion practice.

♦ Ask learners, "What kinds of invitations do you extend to people?"
♦ Do a *roundrobin* and write learners' responses to the question on the board.
♦ Have learners work in mixed-ability groups to sort their responses into two categories: invitations that are oral and invitations that are written.
♦ Debrief using *teams share*.

IN YOUR COMMUNITY

Before learners complete this section of the *worktext,* do a survey. Ask learners to raise their hands if their answers are *yes*.

Do you have any travel brochures at home?
Did you get the brochure from a travel agent?
Did you get the brochure from a friend?
Did you write for the brochure?
Did you call a toll-free number to get the brochure?
Have you ever used a travel brochure to take a vacation?

After the survey, show examples of travel brochures you have collected and talk about where you got each one. Show learners ads with toll-free numbers to call for brochures, coupons to fill out and mail in for information, and brochures you picked up from friends or travel agents. If you have collected enough sample postcards, have learners fill them out for practice completing forms.

After learners have completed the pages in the *worktext,* have them do **Handout 23-B**. Handout 23-B provides reading and conversation practice. Learners role-play telephone calls asking for travel information.

Extension Activity #2 provides additional conversation practice. Joe's son's cabin in the mountains is only a two-hour drive from Crossroads Café. Ask learners to think about places to visit in your state that are a two-hour drive away.

♦ Hang a large map of your state on the wall or make photocopies of a state map for learners.
♦ Circle your city.
♦ Draw another circle that includes places within a two-hour driving radius from your city.
♦ Make a list of places two hours away that learners have been to or where they would like to visit.
♦ Encourage learners to visit these places if they can and report back to the rest of the class.

READ AND WRITE

After learners have completed this section of the *worktext,* have them do a ***think-pair-share*** about birthdays. Use these questions or make up your own. **Debrief** by having a class discussion.

> *Have you ever been to a surprise party?*
> *Who was the party for?*
> *Was the person surprised?*
> *Have you ever given a surprise birthday party for someone?*
> *Who was the person?*
> *Was the person surprised?*

Play Story Clip # 2 and use the ***culture comparison*** video technique.

STORY CLIP #2

TIME CODES: 22:58–25:06   **COUNTER TIMES:**

SCENE: Mr. Brashov finally celebrates his birthday.

FIRST LINE: MR. BRASHOV: Today, I found out that a birthday is just another day . . .

LAST LINE: ALL: Happy Birthday!

While learners watch the clip, ask them to think about how people celebrate birthdays in their native countries.

♦ Make a chart like this one on the board.

COUNTRY	CELEBRATION YES NO	PARTY?	GIFTS?	CARDS?

♦ Ask learners to copy the chart on their own papers.
♦ Divide learners into same-ability groups and have them fill in the chart.
♦ Use ***teams share*** to debrief.

WHAT DO YOU THINK?

After learners have completed this section of the *worktext,* **play Story Clip #3** and use the ***thinking and feeling*** video technique.

While learners are watching the clip, ask them to watch for the answers to these questions. Play the clip again and ask learners to look for support for their answers.

How does Anna feel when she sees her father?
What is Anna thinking when she asks her father how he found her?
How does Mr. Brashov feel when Anna says, "Happy Birthday"?
How does Mr. Brashov feel when he learns his granddaughter's name?
What is Anna thinking when her father says, "I want my daughter back"?

Handout 23-C is a *problem-solving* activity. Learners read and discuss problems related to birthdays.

▶ CULTURE CLIP

Replay **Culture Clip** (10:48–12:47) **before** learners complete the culture pages in the *worktext*. **While** learners watch the clip, have them make a list of the different kinds of taxes mentioned in the clip. Debrief in a class discussion.

- Write THERE'S ONLY TWO THINGS PEOPLE HAVE TO DO—DIE AND PAY TAXES on the board.
- Do a *sides activity.*
- Have learners who agree move to one side of the room and those who disagree move to the other side.
- Give each side time to discuss their reasons.

Handout 23-D is an interview about taxes.

▶ EPISODE WRAP UP

Have a class discussion about the title of this episode, "The Gift."

- Write THE GIFT on the board.
- Ask learners, "Which gift was the title about?"
- Have learners share their reasons with the class.

Encourage learners to write in their journals about a special gift they have received.

ROLE-PLAY

HANDOUT 23-A

Mr. Brashov invited his employees to have dinner with him. They refused because they were going to have a surprise party for him. Practice making invitations.

♦ Work with a partner or in a small group.
♦ Write two more invitations on the blank cards.
♦ Cut the cards and scramble them. Put them face down in a pile.
♦ Take turns. Turn over a card and show it to a partner.
♦ Make invitations and accept or decline them using the examples in YOUR NEW LANGUAGE on page 132 of the *worktext*.

> EXAMPLE: *Go to a concert.*
> A: *Would you like to go to a jazz concert tomorrow night?*
> B: *I'm sorry, but I have to work tomorrow night.*
> A: *Well, maybe we can go another time.*
> B: *Sure. I'd like that.*

----

go to a concert/decline	go hiking in the country/accept
go to a shopping mall/decline	go to an art museum/decline
have a picnic in the park/accept	have lunch at a new restaurant/accept
go to an amusement park/decline	go to a baseball game/decline
go to a health club to exercise/accept	go see a movie/accept
go bicycle riding/decline	play cards/decline

DISCUSSION

HANDOUT 23-B

Mr. Brashov took a vacation at a cabin in the mountains. Where would you like to go on vacation? Read these six ads for vacations from a magazine.

♦ Work with a partner or in a small group.
♦ Choose the vacation ad that interests you the most.
♦ Work together to write questions and answers about the ad.
♦ Role-play a telephone call for information about the vacation place.
♦ Share the role-play with the class.

AD #1
Cruise the Mississippi
• houseboats
• 3-10 day cruises

call (800) 555-7742 for information

AD #2
Bike Tours
Name the state—
we'll make arrangements
Have fun & excercise too!

call (800) 111-2220

AD #3
Midwest Raft & Canoe Trips
• easy to advanced
• reasonable prices

call (800) 999-1231 for information

AD #4
Mall of America
• transportation
• lodging
• 1 meal deal

call (888) 778-4449

AD #5
Niagara Falls
• Maid of the Mist
• Cave of the Winds
• Museums
• Shopping

call (800) 741-0002

AD #6
Hike the Appalachians
• Camp, fish
• Bird watch
• Guide available

call Jim – (800) 928-5643

QUESTIONS	ANSWERS
1.	
2.	
3.	
4.	
5.	

PROBLEM-SOLVING

HANDOUT 23-C

Mr. Brashov's friends and employees have a big problem. They want to surprise Mr. Brashov.

- ◆ Work with a partner or in a small group.
- ◆ Cut the cards.
- ◆ Read the problems on the cards.
- ◆ Write one more problem.
- ◆ Choose one problem to discuss.
- ◆ Share your solutions with the class.

PROBLEM #1   It is your first week at a new job. Tomorrow is one of your coworker's birthdays. You are asked to contribute $10.00 for a gift, card, and cake. You want your new co-workers to like you, but you are not comfortable giving $10.00 for a stranger's party.

SOLUTION:

PROBLEM #2   You gave a very expensive birthday gift to one of your friends. Now it is your birthday. But your friend doesn't give you a gift—only a card. You are very disappointed.

SOLUTION:

PROBLEM #3   A friend gave you a sweater for your birthday. It didn't fit, and you didn't like the color or style. You exchanged the sweater for a different one, but you didn't tell your friend. Your friend asks why you never wear the sweater.

SOLUTION:

PROBLEM #4   You have been invited to a surprise party for one of your neighbors. Your neighbor's husband tells you to bring a joke gift. You don't know what a joke gift is, and you are embarrassed to ask.

SOLUTION:

PROBLEM #5

SOLUTION:

COMPARE CULTURES

HANDOUT 23-D

Mr. Brashov worries about a letter from the Internal Revenue Service (IRS). Do you ever worry about taxes?

- ◆ Interview a partner about taxes.
- ◆ Ask the questions below or make up your own questions.
- ◆ Write your partner's answers on the lines.
- ◆ Share the interview with another pair.

 -

NAME:	INTERVIEWER:
1. Is there a federal income tax in your native country?	
2. Do you think taxes in the United States are higher or lower than in your native country? Why or why not?	
3. How are taxes different in your native country than in the United States? How are taxes the same?	
4. What day are taxes due in your native country?	
5. Do you know anyone who has had tax problems? What happened?	
6. Do people in your native country pay city or state income taxes?	
7. What things should people pay taxes on?	
8. What things shouldn't people pay taxes on?	

UNIT 23 THE GIFT

Katherine, Rosa, and Jamal are in the café. Katherine and Rosa are organizing things for a party.

Mr. Brashov arrives. "What a beautiful day," he says. Rosa says, "It's a very special day." Mr. Brashov is happy. He thinks Rosa remembered his birthday. But Rosa doesn't say, "Happy Birthday." She says, "Today is special because Jamal is going to fix the ice maker." Mr. Brashov is very sad. Nobody remembered his birthday.

A customer comes in the café. His name is Joe. Mr. Brashov hasn't seen Joe for awhile. Joe was at his son's cabin in the mountains. Joe shows Mr. Brashov some pictures. He tells Mr. Brashov to take a vacation.

Jamal is in the utility room. He is putting party decorations in his locker. Mr. Brashov walks in. Jamal tries to hide what he is doing. He doesn't want Mr. Brashov to know about the party. Fortunately, the phone rings. Mr. Brashov picks up the phone and says hello. But no one answers.

Joe comes back to the café with the keys to his son's cabin. He invites Mr. Brashov to the cabin. It's only two hours away. Mr. Brashov can go after work. When Katherine and Rose hear this, they are worried. If Mr. Brashov goes to the cabin, he will miss the surprise birthday party. Mr. Brashov leaves the café with Joe.

Jess and Katherine are in the utility room. Jess is typing a letter from the Internal Revenue Service (IRS) to give to Mr. Brashov. When Mr. Brashov returns to the café, Katherine gives him the mail.

Mr. Brashov sees a letter from the IRS. Someone from the IRS is coming to the café on Monday to see Mr. Brashov's tax records. Now Mr. Brashov cannot go to the cabin.

Jess has a solution to the problem. Mr. Brashov can call Emery Bradford to help him. If Emery and Mr. Brashov work on the tax records tonight, Mr. Brashov can go to the cabin on Saturday.

Emery comes to the café. Mr. Brashov is very depressed. This is not a very happy birthday for him. The phone rings again. It's Nicolae. He' s calling to say "Happy Birthday" to his brother.

Mr. Brashov hangs up the phone. He calls information to get the number for the airport. He leaves the café. When Emery looks for Mr. Brashov, he can't find him. The door to the café opens. Everyone is there for Mr. Brashov's surprise party. But Mr. Brashov is not there!

Mr. Brashov is at the airport. His daughter, Anna, works at the ticket counter. She is very surprised to see her father. She hasn't seen him for a long time. Anna and Mr. Brashov talk.

Suddenly, Mr. Brashov sees his friends from the café. They want Mr. Brashov to return to the café for his surprise birthday party. Jess invites Anna to come, too, but she says she can't.

Back at the café, Mr. Brashov finally celebrates his birthday. There is a cake and gifts. And one gift is very special. Anna comes to the café—with her daughter, Elizabeth. For the first time, Mr. Brashov meets his granddaughter. Mr. Brashov finally has a very happy birthday.

UNIT 24 ALL'S WELL THAT ENDS WELL

TEACHER'S NOTES AT A GLANCE

	ACTIVITIES	MATERIALS	TIME
CLASS OPENER	◆ discussion		5–10 minutes
YOUR NEW LANGUAGE	*Do before worktext* ◆ replay **Word Play** ◆ brainstorming ◆ play **Story Clip #1** ◆ language practice	TV/VCR board Handout 24-A Handout 24-B	2–5 minutes 10–15 minutes 10–15 minutes 15–20 minutes
IN YOUR COMMUNITY	*Do after worktext* ◆ matching ◆ survey/reading practice	Handout 24-C engagement, wedding, and anniversary announcements from newspapers, transparencies, photocopies	20–30 minutes 15–45 minutes
READ AND WRITE	*Do after worktext* ◆ 3-step interview	board	15–20 minutes
WHAT DO YOU THINK?	*Do after worktext* ◆ play **Story Clip #2**	TV/VCR	10–15 minutes
CULTURE CLIP	*Do before worktext* ◆ replay **Culture Clip** ◆ interview ◆ play **Story Clip #3**	TV/VCR Handout 24-D TV/VCR	2–5 minutes 20–30 minutes 5–10 minutes
EPISODE WRAP UP	◆ brainstorming ◆ journal writing	board	10–15 minutes

VIDEO HIGHLIGHTS	
19:11–20:39	**Word Play:** Talking about the future.
8:01–10:20	**Culture Clip:** Wedding customs
1:16–2:23	**Story Clip #1:** Everyone at Crossroads Café is getting ready for Bill and Katherine's dinner party.
14:00–15:23	**Story Clip #2:** Bill's family mistakes Rosa for Katherine.
15:26–16:50	**Story Clip #3:** Henry picks up the wrong man at the airport.

▶ CLASS OPENER

See suggestions on page xii of the Introduction.

▶ YOUR NEW LANGUAGE

Replay **Word Play** (19:11–20:39) **before** learners complete this section of the *worktext*. Introduce the language focus.

- ♦ Make a chart like this one on the board.
- ♦ Divide learners into mixed-ability groups.
- ♦ Have the groups brainstorm two lists—one list of things Katherine and Bill **will** do on their wedding day, the other a list of things their guests **are going to** do.
- ♦ Debrief using **best idea** only.

THINGS KATHERINE AND BILL WILL DO	THINGS GUESTS ARE GOING TO DO

Handout 24-A provides active listening practice and reviews the language focus. Play **Story Clip #1 while** learners put the cards in order.

STORY CLIP #1

TIME CODES: 1:16–2:23   **COUNTER TIMES:**

SCENE: Everyone at the café is getting ready for Bill and Katherine's dinner party.

FIRST LINE: ROSA: Okay, let's synchronize our watches.

LAST LINE: ROSA: Here you go.

After learners have completed Handout 24-A, ask them which card uses will, but doesn't refer to the future (Will one of you lucky girls please give me a signature?). Ask learners what other words they could use in place of *will* (can, would, etc.).

Handout 24-B provides additional practice using the future.

▶ IN YOUR COMMUNITY

After learners have completed the pages in the *worktext,* have them complete **Handout 24-C**. This activity provides learners with an opportunity to discuss gift giving for special occasions. Stress to learners that there are no right or wrong matches. The purpose of this activity is to encourage discussion.

If there is time, do **Extension Activity #1.** Collect engagement, wedding, and anniversary announcements from the newspaper. Survey learners about their familiarity with announcements before they do the following activity. Ask learners to raise their hands if their answers are yes.

> *Have ever you read a <u>wedding</u> announcement in the newspaper?*
>
> *Have you ever placed a <u>wedding</u> announcement in the newspaper?* (Substitute engagement and anniversary for the underlined words.)

Then do the following.

- ◆ Make transparencies of the announcements for yourself and photocopies of the announcements for learners.
- ◆ Divide class into same-ability learner groups.
- ◆ Give each group a set of announcements.
- ◆ Ask each group of learners to write 3–5 questions about the announcements.
- ◆ Have learners exchange their announcements and questions with another group.

▶ READ AND WRITE

After learners have completed this section of the *worktext,* do a *3-step-interview*. Write these questions on the board. Debrief in a large class discussion.

> *Do you write thank-you notes?*
>
> *Who would you like to write a thank-you note to?*
>
> *When do you write thank-you notes?*
>
> *Do you receive thank-you notes?*
>
> *When do you receive thank-you notes?*
>
> *How do you feel when you receive thank-you notes?*
>
> *How do you feel when you don't receive thank-you notes?*
>
> *Do people in your native country usually write thank-you notes?*

A variation is to do a *sides activity* about thank-you notes. Have those who write them move to one side of the room, and those who don't move to the other side. Both sides can discuss their reasons and share them with the class.

▶ WHAT DO YOU THINK?

After learners have completed this section of the *worktext,* play **Story Clip #2** and use the *watchers and listeners* video technique.

STORY CLIP #2

TIME CODES: 14:00–15:23   **COUNTER TIMES:**

SCENE: Bill's family mistakes Rosa for Katherine.

FIRST LINE: MR. BRASHOV: Welcome, welcome. Come in. It's nice to meet you.

LAST LINE: JESS: Look at it this way. Your family isn't losing a son. It's gaining two daughters.

Write these questions on the board for learners to answer **after** you have played the clip.

Who is the first person to mistake Rosa for Katherine?

Why doesn't Rosa tell anyone she is not Katherine?

Why don't Mr. Brashov, Jess, and Jamal say anything?

What does Bill's family say about Rosa?

Who starts playing music?

What do the people do when they hear the music?

CULTURE CLIP

Replay **Culture Clip** (8:01–10:20) **before** learners complete this section of the *worktext*. While learners are watching the clip, have them make a list of wedding customs that are the same in many cultures. After the clip, have a discussion about the lists. Ask learners to share information about wedding customs in their cultures. Ask learners to bring wedding pictures to class to share.

Handout 24-D is an *interview* about weddings. Debrief the interviews in a large class discussion.

Play Story Clip #3 and use the *culture comparison* video technique. In this clip, Henry has picked up the wrong man at the airport.

STORY CLIP #3

TIME CODES: 15:26–16:50   **COUNTER TIMES:**

SCENE: Henry picks up the wrong man at the airport.

FIRST LINE: HENRY: Are you waiting for a ride?

LAST LINE: HENRY & CALLI: Uh, oh.

While learners watch the clip, ask them to think about these questions.

Why did Henry think the man was Katherine's grandfather?

How did Henry realize his mistake?

Why did the man go with Henry?

Would this happen in your native country? Why or why not?

Has anything like this ever happened to you

What advice do you have for Henry so he can avoid mistakes like this in the future?

After the clip, have learners discuss their answers with partners and use ***teams share*** to debrief.

EPISODE WRAP UP

Before learners complete **Check Your English**, have a discussion about the title of this episode, "All's Well That Ends Well."

- Write the title on the board.
- Ask learners to brainstorm a list of everything that went wrong in this episode.
- Go one by one down the list and ask learners to tell how each problem was resolved.
- Ask learners to explain what the title means.
- Ask learners to share any similar expressions in their native languages and write these on the board.
- Encourage learners to write in their journals about times when everything seemed to go wrong, but all turned out well in the end.

DIALOGUE

HANDOUT 24-A

Everyone at the café is getting ready for Bill and Katherine's party. What are they going to do?

♦ Work with a partner.
♦ Read the dialogue cards below.
♦ Cut the cards and scramble them. Put them face up.
♦ Put the dialogue cards in order while you watch the story clip.
♦ Share with another pair. Is the order of the cards the same?

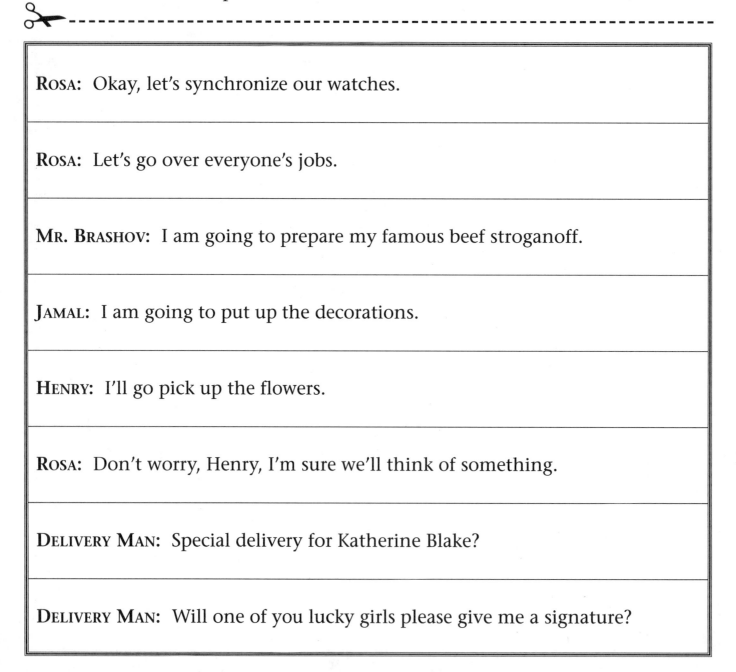

ROSA: Okay, let's synchronize our watches.

ROSA: Let's go over everyone's jobs.

MR. BRASHOV: I am going to prepare my famous beef stroganoff.

JAMAL: I am going to put up the decorations.

HENRY: I'll go pick up the flowers.

ROSA: Don't worry, Henry, I'm sure we'll think of something.

DELIVERY MAN: Special delivery for Katherine Blake?

DELIVERY MAN: Will one of you lucky girls please give me a signature?

ROLE-PLAY

HANDOUT 24-B

People use ***going to*** or ***will*** to talk about the future. What's in your future?

♦ Work with a partner.
♦ Each person writes a future expression and time on two blank cards.
♦ Cut the cards and scramble them. Put them face down in a pile.
♦ Take turns turning over the cards and role-play the situations.

> EXAMPLE: *going to/this afternoon*
> A: *What are you going to do this afternoon?*
> B: *I'm going to visit my aunt.*

♦ Share one role-play with the rest of the class.

✂ -

going to/this afternoon	going to/tomorrow morning
will/tomorrow night	will/ next week
going to/tonight	going to /next month
will/next winter	will /next spring
going to/next fall	going to/tomorrow afternoon
going to/tomorrow night	will/Saturday
will/on Sunday	will/in two weeks

MATCH UP

HANDOUT 24-C

What gifts did Bill and Katherine receive for their wedding? Think about the gifts people give on special occasions.

♦ Work with a partner or in a small group.
♦ Cut the cards and scramble them. Turn them face up.
♦ Match the gifts with the occasion.
♦ Share your cards with another pair or group. Are they the same or different?

- -

crystal vase	housewarming
silver comb and brush set	new baby
silver comb and brush set	baby shower
bed sheets	wedding shower
$100.00	wedding gift
microwave oven	engagement gift
watch	high school graduation gift
car	college graduation
crystal table clock	10th anniversary

INTERVIEW

HANDOUT 24-D

Katherine and Bill are getting married.

♦ Interview someone about a wedding he or she attended.
♦ Ask the questions below, and add two more questions.
♦ Write the answers to the questions on the lines.
♦ Ask for permission to share the interview with the rest of the class.

NAME:	INTERVIEWER:
1. When was the last wedding you attended?	
2. Who were the bride and groom?	
3. How well did you know the bride and groom?	
4. Where was the wedding?	
5. What kind of dress did the bride wear? What did the groom wear?	
6. How many people were in the bridal party? What did they wear?	
7. How many people attended the wedding?	
8. Was there a reception (party)? What kind of food did you eat? Was there dancing?	
9. What gift did you give the bride and groom?	
10. Did you have fun at the wedding? Why or why not?	
11.	
12.	

UNIT 24 ALL'S WELL THAT ENDS WELL

It's snowing and Crossroads Café is closed. Jamal, Henry, Mr. Brashov, and Jess are looking at their watches. Rosa has a clipboard. She says to the men, "Let's synchronize our watches." Mr. Brashov and Rosa are having a dinner party for Katherine and Bill in four hours, forty-five minutes, and seventeen seconds. They are getting married tomorrow.

Everyone has a job to do except Henry. Mr. Brashov is making beef stroganoff. Jamal is putting up decorations. Carol is picking up the flowers.

A delivery man comes in the café with a box for Katherine. It's her wedding dress. Rosa opens the box to check on the dress. Oh no! The dress is the wrong size. It's huge. It's big enough for two or three Katherines to wear. Henry says, "Katherine had better start eating."

Henry goes outside to check the weather. It's snowing very hard. Rosa is worried about Katherine's grandfather. He is flying in from Europe, and someone has to pick him up at the airport.

There is another problem. Rosa hears Suzanne and David arguing in the kitchen. They were helping Rosa make pastries and Suzanne lost her mother's wedding ring!

Katherine and Bill enter the café. They are very happy. But when Katherine greets her children, Suzanne starts to cry and runs out of the room.

Everyone tells Katherine about the problems. Katherine is not happy any more. She asks about her wedding dress and decides to try it on. Katherine locks herself in the bathroom and cries after she sees the dress. She won't talk to anyone. She just cries.

Mr. Brashov tries to call the airport for information about flights from Europe. Everyone, except for Katherine, is listening to the radio. The weather is getting worse.

Finally, there is a job for Henry. Mr. Brashov decides to send Henry to the airport to pick up Katherine's grandfather. He gives Henry money for a taxi. Katherine gives Henry a description of her grandfather so Henry will recognize him.

Bill's family starts to arrive at the café for the dinner party. Bill's Uncle Antonio sees Rosa and calls her Katherine. He welcomes her to the family. Rosa is so surprised, she can't speak.

Henry has several problems at the airport. First, he picks up the wrong man. Then he finds the right man, but the taxi has a flat tire on the way back to Crossroads Café. Katherine's grandfather changes the tire.

Back at the café, Bill tells his family Rosa is not Katherine. Jamal says, "Katherine is at home. She's checking on her wedding dress." Bill's family doesn't know Katherine is in the utility room. She is a mess because she is crying.

Jamal helps Katherine climb out a window. Then she enters the café again— through the front door. Everyone is very happy to finally meet the bride!

The bride is happy, too. Her grandfather comes in with Henry and the taxi driver, and the party begins. When they all sit down to eat, Aunt Sophie finds the missing wedding ring in a pastry. All's well that ends well!

UNIT 25 COMINGS AND GOINGS

TEACHER'S NOTES
AT A GLANCE

	ACTIVITIES	MATERIALS	TIME
CLASS OPENER	◆ discussion		5–10 minutes
YOUR NEW LANGUAGE	*Do before worktext* ◆ replay **Word Play** ◆ think-pair-share ◆ Johari Window ◆ sides activity (Ext. Act. #1)	TV/VCR board Handout 25-A	2–5 minutes 5–10 minutes 15–20 minutes 10–15 minutes
IN YOUR COMMUNITY	*Do after worktext* ◆ play **Story Clip #1** ◆ problem-solving	TV/VCR Handout 25-B	10–15 minutes 10–15 minutes
READ AND WRITE	*Do after worktext* ◆ 3-step interview ◆ writing activity (Ext. Act. #2)	board board	10–15 minutes 20–30 minutes
WHAT DO YOU THINK?	*Do before worktext* ◆ play **Story Clip #2** ◆ discussion	TV/VCR Handout 25-C	10–15 minutes 15–20 minutes
CULTURE CLIP	*Do before worktext* ◆ replay **Culture Clip** ◆ conversation practice	TV/VCR Handout 25-D	2–5 minutes 15–20 minutes
EPISODE WRAP UP	◆ play **Story Clip #3** ◆ discussion ◆ journal writing	TV/VCR board	5–10 minutes 5–10 minutes

VIDEO HIGHLIGHTS	
16:57–18:26	**Word Play:** Talking about definite and indefinite plans
9:59–11:48	**Culture Clip:** Returning to your home culture
18:28–19:28	**Story Clip #1:** Henry is in Danny's office the day after the concert at Crossroads Café.
8:26–9:57	**Story Clip #2:** Abdullah offers Jamal a job—in Egypt.
22:13–24:49	**Story Clip #3:** Everyone is at Katherine's farewell party.

CLASS OPENER

See suggestions on page xii of the Introduction.

YOUR NEW LANGUAGE

Replay **Word Play** (16:57-18:26) **before** learners complete this section of the *worktext*. Introduce the language focus.

- Ask learners to do a ***think-pair share*** about their plans for the rest of the day or evening (after class).
- Make a chart like this one on the board and ask learners to copy it on their papers.

THINGS I'M DEFINITELY GOING TO DO	THINGS I MIGHT DO

- Have learners list 3-to-5 things in each column.
- Debrief in a whole class discussion.
- Have learners take turns asking each other, *"What are you definitely going to do today (or this evening)?* and *What do you think you might do today (or this evening)?*
- Write learners' responses on the board while they are speaking.

After learners have completed the pages in the *worktext,* have them complete **Handout 25-A. Handout 25-A** is a *Johari Window.* It provides learners with additional opportunities to practice the language used for talking about plans. Have each pair share its answers with another pair or the rest of the class since learners' responses may give you ideas for future lessons.

Extension Activity #1 is a ***sides activity.*** Use the following sentences or make up your own. After each statement, learners move to one side of the room if they are sure the event or situation is going to happen and the other side of the room if they think it might happen. Give learners time to share their reasons before you go on to the next statement.

> *Henry is going to be a rock star.*
> *Katherine is going to be a successful lawyer.*
> *Rosa is going to own her own restaurant.*
> *Jamal is going to be an engineer again.*
> *Mr. Brashov is going to sell Crossroads Café.*
> *Jess is going to beat Mr. Brashov at chess.*

IN YOUR COMMUNITY

After learners have completed the pages in the *worktext,* **play Story Clip #1** and use the ***behavior study*** video technique. Danny advises Henry to go to college.

TIME CODES: 18:28–19:28   **COUNTER TIMES:**

SCENE: Henry is in Danny's office the day after the concert.

FIRST LINE: HENRY: I don't get it.

LAST LINE: DANNY: Good luck, Henry.

While learners are watching the clip, have them look for the answers to the following questions.

> *Why is Henry upset? How can you tell he is upset?*
>
> *Why doesn't Henry like Danny's advice to go to college?*
>
> *How can you tell Henry doesn't like this advice?*
>
> *How does Henry feel about Danny now? How can you tell?*

Handout 25-B provides learners with opportunities to read and discuss class descriptions. Debrief by having a discussion about the lifelong learning opportunities in the learners' communities. Collect class schedules and course descriptions to share with the class. Your local library is a good source for such information.

▶ READ AND WRITE

After learners have completed this section of the *worktext,* do a *3-step interview* about thank-you notes. Write these questions on the board or make up your own.

> *Have you ever written a thank-you note to anyone?*
>
> *Why did you write a thank-you note?*
>
> *Did you buy a special card or stationery?*
>
> *Do people write thank-you notes in your native country?*
>
> *Have you ever given your boss a gift to say thank you or for a special occasion? What was the gift? What did your boss do?*
>
> *Do people give gifts to their bosses in your native country? When?*

Extension Activity #2 provides learners with opportunities to write thank-you notes to Mr. Brashov from the viewpoints of the Crossroads Café characters.

♦ Make a chart like the one below on the board.

PERSON	REASONS FOR THANK-YOU NOTES
Jamal	
Henry	
Rosa	
Marie	

♦ Brainstorm a class list of reasons why characters might write thank-you notes to Mr. Brashov.

♦ Have learners write thank-you notes from one person listed on the board.

♦ Have learners volunteer to share their notes if they agree.

WHAT DO YOU THINK?

Before learners complete this section of the *worktext,* **play Story Clip #2** and use the *freeze frame* technique.

> STORY CLIP #2
>
> **TIME CODES:** 8:26–9:57 and   **COUNTER TIMES:**
> 11:53–12:58
>
> **SCENE:** Abdullah offers Jamal a job—in Egypt.
>
> **FIRST LINE:** ABDULLAH: That was a wonderful meal.
>
> **LAST LINE:** JAMAL: I cannot do this anymore.

♦ Use the pause button to focus learners' attention on Jamal in the following scenes. When . . .

1. the baby cries and Jamal and Jihan exchange looks. (Ask, *What does the look mean?*)
2. Abdullah offers Jamal a job. (Ask, *What is Jamal's reaction?*)
3. Jamal tells Jihan to sit down. (Ask, *Why do Jamal and Abdullah look at each other?*)
4. Jamal and Jihan are eating breakfast the next morning. (Ask, *What's wrong between Jihan and Jamal?*)
5. Jamal tells Jihan, "I cannot do this anymore." (Ask, *How does Jamal feel?*)

Handout 25-C is a discussion activity. Learners predict the future for the characters at Crossroads Café and discuss their predictions with their partners. Debrief by making a class chart of the number or percent of yes answers for each question.

CULTURE CLIP

Replay **Culture Clip** (9:59–11:48) **before** learners complete this section of the *worktext.* **While** learners are watching the clip, ask them to fill in the chart. Draw a chart like this one on the board, and have learners copy it on their papers.

NAME	COUNTRY	REASONS
Rader Faroush		
Nils Vuong		
Juan Franco		
Edgar Villarmarin		

After learners have watched the clip, have them share their charts with their partners. Are they the same? Debrief in a large class discussion.

Handout 25-D provides conversation practice. Learners discuss reasons for staying in the United States or leaving. Debrief in a large class discussion.

- Begin the discussion by asking learners to raise their hands if they have ever wanted to return to their native countries.
- Ask learners who said *yes* to share their reasons with the class.
- Ask learners to work with a partner to role-play a discussion between someone who wants to leave the United States and someone who wants that person to stay.
- Ask learners to share their role-plays with another pair.
- Have each small group share one role-play with the class.

▶ EPISODE WRAP UP

Before learners discuss the title of this episode, **play Story Clip #3** and use the *telling the story* video technique.

STORY CLIP #3

TIME CODES: 22:13–24:49   **COUNTER TIMES:**

SCENE: Katherine's farewell party.

FIRST LINE: KATHERINE: This is a wonderful party Mr. Brashov.

LAST LINE: MR. BRASHOV: Jess died about an hour ago.

Have a class discussion about the title of this episode.

- Write COMINGS AND GOINGS on the board.
- Ask learners, "Who came?" and write their responses on the board under COMING.
- Ask learners, "What were the 'goings'?" and write their responses on the board under GOINGS.
- Have learners share their feelings about the ending of this episode with a partner or a small group.
- Encourage learners to write in their journals about people in their lives who have come and gone.

TALK ABOUT THE FUTURE

HANDOUT 25-A

Katherine is planning to go back to college. Jamal and Jihan are planning to return to Egypt. Think about your plans for the future.

- Work with a partner.
- Fill in the boxes with information about your plans for the future.
- Share the information with another pair or the class.

Both of us are definitely planning to . . .	A might . . .
B might . . .	Neither of us is planning to . . .

PROBLEM-SOLVING

HANDOUT 25-B

Katherine is going back to college. In addition to taking college classes, many adults take classes at other places such as park districts or community centers.

- ♦ Work with a partner or in a small group.
- ♦ Read the class descriptions below.
- ♦ Decide which classes each of the Crossroads Café characters might take.
- ♦ Give your reasons why the character would take the class.
- ♦ Choose one class you might be interested in and give your reasons.
- ♦ Share your choices and reasons with the class.

Cooking Around the World This class will teach you how to make a five-course meal from a country on every one of the seven continents. Tuesday: 7:00–10:00 P.M. Five weeks beginning 10/14 $65.00	**Advanced Guitar** Improve your technique and write music in this fast-paced class. The instructor is a professional who has played guitar in several well-known bands. Wednesday: 8:00–9:30 P.M. 10 weeks beginning 10/15 $100.00
Financial Planning for Retirement Now is the perfect time to plan your retirement. Will you have enough money to do what you want? How much money will you need? What kind of health insurance do you need? These and other questions will be answered in this class. Monday: 6:30–8:30 P.M. Four weeks beginning 10/13 $55.00	**Step-Parenting** Marriage is hard work, especially if you have stepchildren. Learn how to avoid problems with stepchildren and develop healthy, loving relationships with them. Thursday: 7:00–8:30 P.M. Three weeks beginning 11/16 $30.00
Tips for Running a Successful Business Want to own your own business or just thinking about it? Chances are you don't know everything you need to know. Get advice from a trio of successful businessmen and women. You'll save time and money! Wednesday: 7:00–9:00 P.M. Five weeks beginning 11/1 $65.00	**Study Skills for Adults** Is returning to school in your future? Learn how to manage your time effectively, organize class notes, use the Internet to do research, and review for tests. Thursday: 8:00–9:30 P.M. Four weeks beginning 11/2 $40.00

INTERVIEW

HANDOUT 25-C

What's going to happen to the people at Crossroads Café?

- ◆ Read the questions.
- ◆ Check YES or NO for each question.
- ◆ Write two more questions in the blanks.
- ◆ Compare your answers with a partner. Are your answers the same or different? Give reasons for your answers.
- ◆ Share your answers with the class.

	YES	NO
1. Is Mr. Brashov going to slow down?		
2. Is Henry planning to go to college?		
3. Is Henry going to be a famous rock star some day?		
4. Is Mr. Brashov going to get a new chess partner?		
5. Is Jamal going to go back to Egypt?		
6. Is Jihan going to be happy in Egypt?		
7. Is Katherine going to be a lawyer?		
8. Is Henry going to give any more concerts at Crossroads Café?		
9. Will Rosa and Marie become friends?		
10. Will Katherine and Rosa remain friends?		
11.		
12.		

REASONS

HANDOUT 25-D

Millions of people come to the United States each year. Many stay here. Some, like Jamal and Jihan, return to their native countries. Think about why some people stay and other people leave.

♦ Work with a partner or in a small group.
♦ Read the cards.
♦ Each partner adds *one reason for* **staying** and *one reason for* **returning** *home.*
♦ Cut the cards and scramble them.
♦ Discuss the cards and put them in two columns: *reasons for* **staying** *in the United States* and *reasons for* **returning** *home.*
♦ Share your answers with the class.

a good job	cost of living
educational opportunities	medical care
chance to own a business	friends and family
high level of technology	own property
war in native country	crime
variety of people	culture
freedom of religion	language
spouse and children are citizens	government

COMINGS AND GOINGS

Rosa is speaking Spanish to some customers. When Katherine comes to take their order, she speaks Spanish, too. Rosa says, "Congratulations. I almost understood you."

Jamal asks Katherine about her plans for the future. Katherine is leaving Crossroads Café to spend time with her children, help her husband, and go back to school. Katherine wants to be a lawyer. Rosa laughs and says, "That is a perfect job for you!"

Mr. Brashov has one last task for Katherine. He wants her to hire the new waitress. This worries Rosa.

Henry is in the office of a record producer, Danny. Henry wants to be a rock star. The producer listens to a tape of Henry and his band. They sound good, but the producer wants to hear them play in person. Henry invites Danny to a live concert at Crossroads Café.

The next day at the café, Jamal gets a phone call. It's a friend from Egypt. Jamal's friend, Abdullah, is in town and Jamal invites him for dinner.

Katherine interviews waitresses. She talks to many applicants, but she doesn't hire anyone. Rosa, Jess, and Mr. Brashov don't understand Katherine. There are many qualified people, but Katherine is still looking.

Jess wants to play chess with Mr. Brashov, but Mr. Brashov has too much work to do. He promises to play chess with Jess on Friday.

Henry tells Katherine about Danny. He is coming to Crossroads Café to hear Henry play. There's only one problem. Henry has to ask Mr. Brashov for permission to have a concert at the café. Mr. Brashov is not enthusiastic, but he agrees.

It's night. Jamal is eating dinner at home with Abdullah, his friend from Egypt. Abdullah's company needs a chief engineer. Abdullah offers Jamal a job in Egypt.

Jihan is surprised to learn Jamal wants to return to Egypt. Jihan likes her job, and she is happy in the United States. But Jamal is unhappy. He used to be an engineer, and now he is a handyman. Jamal doesn't want to be a handyman anymore.

The next day, Katherine interviews another applicant for the waitress job, a young Haitian woman, Marie. Rosa asks Katherine, "How was she?" Katherine answers, "Great." But Katherine didn't hire Marie. Katherine's looking for the perfect waitress.

Later in the evening, there is a crowd at the café. Danny, the producer , comes to hear Henry and the band. Henry is happy to see Danny there. But the next day, when he goes to see Danny, Henry is very disappointed. Danny doesn't think Henry is good enough to sign a contract. Danny tells Henry to go to college.

It's Katherine's last day at Crossroads Café. And surprise—the café finally has a new waitress—Marie. Katherine introduces Jess to Marie. Then Jess and Mr. Brashov start to play chess. A delivery man interrupts their game. Jess is disappointed. Mr. Brashov promises to finish the game after Katherine's party.

The café is closed for the day, and the party for Katherine begins. Everyone is there except Carol and Jess. Then the phone rings. It's Carol. She has terrible news. Jess was in a car accident. Jess is dead. Katherine's party is over.

UNIT 26 WINDS OF CHANGE

TEACHER'S NOTES AT A GLANCE

	ACTIVITIES	MATERIALS	TIME
CLASS OPENER	◆ discussion		5–10 minutes
YOUR NEW LANGUAGE	*Do before worktext* ◆ replay **Word Play** ◆ think-pair-share ◆ role-play ◆ brainstorming (Ext. Act. #1)	TV/VCR board Handout 26-A board	2–5 minutes 10–15 minutes 15–20 minutes 10–15 minutes
IN YOUR COMMUNITY	*Do after worktext* ◆ survey ◆ information gap ◆ map making (Ext. Act. #2) ◆ play **Story Clip #1**	 TV/VCR; Handout 26-B paper, colored markers TV/VCR	5 minutes 10–15 minutes 15–30 minutes 10 minutes
READ AND WRITE	◆ write postcards, letters, or eulogy		10–20 minutes
WHAT DO YOU THINK?	*Do before worktext* ◆ play **Story Clip #2** ◆ active listening ◆ sides activity (Ext. Act. #3)	TV/VCR Handout 26-C	2–5 minutes 5–10 minutes 10–20 minutes
CULTURE CLIP	*Do before worktext* ◆ replay **Culture Clip** ◆ interview ◆ panel discussion (Ext. Act. #4)	TV/VCR Handout 26-D	2–5 minutes 15–30 minutes 30–45 minutes
EPISODE WRAP UP	◆ play **Story Clip #3** ◆ discussion ◆ journal writing	TV/VCR board	10–15 minutes 5–15 minutes

VIDEO HIGHLIGHTS	
19:26–20:55	**Word Play:** Expressing obligations
11:43–15:13	**Culture Clip:** Achieving goals
9:41–11:40	**Story Clip #1:** Marie talks to Henry about education while she's giving him first aid.
15:26–17:33	**Story Clip #2:** Carol Washington gives Mr. Brashov tickets for a cruise to the Greek islands.
23:03–25:34	**Story Clip #3:** Mr. Brashov decides not to sell Crossroads Café to Mr. Clayborne.

CLASS OPENER

See suggestions on page xii of the Introduction.

YOUR NEW LANGUAGE

Replay **Word Play** (19:26–20:55) **before** learners complete this section of the *worktext*. Introduce the language focus.

- ◆ Begin by asking a learner what she or he must to do today (tomorrow, the next day, this weekend, etc.) That person asks another learner until everyone in the class has asked and answered the question.
- ◆ Make a chart on the board like this one.

ROSA	JAMAL	MARIE	MR. BRASHOV	HENRY

- ◆ Have learners do a ***think-pair-share*** about things the employees at Crossroads Café must do.
- ◆ Ask learners to think of 3–5 things for each person.
- ◆ Debrief using ***stand-up and share***.
- ◆ Write the learners' ideas in the chart as you debrief.

Handout 26-A is a role-play. While learners practice giving directions for common activities, they use ***have to*** and ***must.***

Extension Activity #1 is a class brainstorming activity.

- ◆ Divide class into ***same-ability*** learner groups.
- ◆ Have each group brainstorm a list of things Mr. Brashov must do before he leaves for his cruise to the Greek islands.
- ◆ Debrief using ***teams share***.

IN YOUR COMMUNITY

After learners have completed this section of the *worktext,* do a hand survey about map reading. Ask these questions or make up your own. Ask learners to raise their hands if their answers are yes. Ask,

> *Do you use maps to find places you are going to?*
> *Do you have a city map at home or in your car?*
> *Do you have a state map at home or in your car?*
> *Can you easily read maps?*
> *Would you rather listen to directions or read a map?*
> *Have you ever been lost?*

Handout 26-B is an *information gap*. Learners ask and answer questions to find the missing information on the maps. Review directions (north, south, east, west) and prepositions of location (next to, across from, in the middle, etc.) before learners do this activity.

Extension Activity #2 provides learners with practice making maps.

- Distribute unlined white paper and colored markers or pencils.
- Ask learners to draw maps of their neighborhoods or the neighborhood around their schools or community centers.
- With learners' permission, post the maps and give learners time to admire each other's work.

A variation is to have learners draw maps from their school to their homes.
Play Story Clip #1 and use the *watchers and listeners* video technique.

STORY CLIP #1

TIME CODES: 9:41–11:40   **COUNTER TIMES:**

SCENE: Marie talks to Henry about education while she's giving him first aid.

FIRST LINE: MARIE: You should be more careful, Henry.

LAST LINE: JAMAL: No. That's when I knew I didn't want to collect garbage.

Write the following questions on the board or make up your own.

What happened to Henry?
Who helped him?
What did this person do?
Who is a nurse?
What education does Henry need to work at Crossroads Café?
Why does Henry talk to Jamal about career goals?

▶ READ AND WRITE

If there is time, **after** learners have completed this section of the *worktext,* have learners complete one of the following writing activities.

- Write postcards from Jamal (back in Egypt) or Mr. Brashov (on cruise) to their friends at Crossroads Café.
- Write a good-bye letter from Jamal to Mr. Brashov.
- Write a good-bye letter from Mr. Brashov (a eulogy) to Jess.

WHAT DO YOU THINK?

After learners have completed this section of the *worktext*, **play Story Clip #2** and use Handout 26-C.

> **STORY CLIP #2**
>
> **TIME CODES:** 15:26–17:33   **COUNTER TIMES:**
>
> **SCENE:** Carol Washington gives Mr. Brashov tickets for a cruise to the Greek islands.
>
> **FIRST LINE:** MR. BRASHOV: Carol, come in.
>
> **Last line:** MR. BRASHOV: All right, for Jess.

Extension Activity #3 is a *sides activity*. Use the following questions or make up your own. Have learners move to one side of the room if their answers to the question are **YES** and the other side of the room if their answers are **NO**. Give learners time to share the reasons for their choices after each question.

> *Should Carol keep the chess set?*
> *Should Mr. Brashov accept the cruise tickets from Carol?*
> *Should he offer to pay Carol for them?*
> *Will Mr. Brashov enjoy the cruise?*
> *Will Rosa be a good manager of the café?*
> *Will Henry work part-time at the café while he goes to college?*
> *Will Henry graduate from college?*

CULTURE CLIP

Replay **Culture Clip** (11:43–15:13) **before** learners complete this section of the *worktext*. Introduce the Culture Clip by telling learners they will be listening to Edgar Villamarin talk about his life in the United States.

- ◆ Ask learners to make a list of 5–7 things Edgar has done since he came to live in the United States.
- ◆ Have learners compare their lists (of things Edgar has done) with their partners.
- ◆ Have learners do pair dictations using their earlier sentences. Everyone begins with this sentence: Edgar Villamarin came to the United States after he graduated from high school in Colombia.
- ◆ Debrief by having learners share their sentences with another pair.

Handout 26-D is an interview. Learners share information about their activities and goals since they came to the United States. With learners' permission, ask them to share their interviews with the class.

Extension Activity #4 is a panel discussion. Invite several former students to participate in a panel discussion about their lives in the United States—activities, goals, what they have "given back," etc.

For variation, invite someone involved with the Big Brothers or Big Sisters organization to class to be interviewed. Have learners prepare questions and practice asking them before the interview.

Have the class write thank-you notes to the visitors.

▶ EPISODE WRAP UP

Before learners discuss the title of this episode, **play Story Clip #3** and use the *behavior study* and *thinking and feeling* video techniques.

STORY CLIP #3

TIME CODES: 23:03–25:34   **COUNTER TIMES:**

SCENE: Mr. Brashov decides not to sell Crossroads Café to Mr. Clayborne.

FIRST LINE: MR. BRASHOV: Thanks for coming in.

LAST LINE: ROSA: Yes!

Stop the clip after each of these dialogue lines and ask learners:

> *What is Mr. Brashov thinking?*
> *What is Rosa feeling?*
> *How do you know?*

1. Mr. Brashov: As it turns out, Rosa, he won't be buying Crossroads Café after all.
2. Mr. Brashov: I know a manager who can run the restaurant for me.
3. Mr. Brashov: If you're going to manage Crossroads Café, you should be able to open the door.
4. Mr. Brashov: And whatever we haven't covered, we can discuss when I return.

End the discussion by asking learners,

> *Why did Rosa say, "Yes!" at the end of the clip?*
> *What else could Rosa have said?*

To end the unit, write WINDS OF CHANGE on the board. Ask learners,

> *What changes took place in this episode?*
> *What does the word **wind** refer to?*
> *What does the title mean?*

To end the series, have a discussion about learners' opinions of the videos, the *worktext* activities, the improvement in learners' English skills, what they've learned about being successful language learners, etc. Also encourage learners to write in their journals about how they feel about their completion of the series.

ROLE-PLAY

HANDOUT 26-A

Before they go to Egypt, Jamal and Jihan have many things to do.

♦ Work with a partner or in a small group.

♦ Read the cards below. Each person writes one or two more things to do on the blank cards.

♦ Cut the cards and scramble them. Put them face down in a pile.

♦ Take turns. Turn over a card. Read the card and say three things you have to do about the topic. Use **have to** and **must**.

♦ Add one more thing to your partner's list.

> EXAMPLE: *Wash dishes*
> A: *You have to turn on the hot water.*
> *You must add soap to the water.*
> *You have to put the dirty dishes in the sink.*
> B: *You must close the drain.*

Wash clothes	Cash a paycheck
Change jobs	Make an appointment with a doctor
Go back to school	Buy a computer
Meet a friend for lunch	Give a party for a friend
Cook your favorite food	Move to a new home
Get a driver's license	Paint the living room

INFORMATION GAP

HANDOUT 26-B

Look at this map of a college campus.   **A**

♦ Work with a partner.

♦ Ask questions to find these places: Classroom Building, Arts Building, Tennis Courts, Parking Lot 7, Parking Lot 8, and Law School.

EXAMPLE: A: *Where's the Classroom Building?*
      B: *It's in the middle of the campus.*

♦ Write the information on the map.

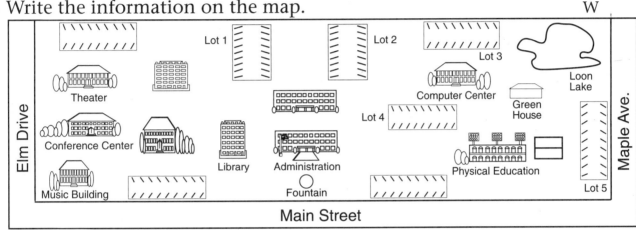

Look at this map of a college campus.   **B**

♦ Work with a partner.

♦ Ask questions to find these places: Music Building, Library, Administration Building, Computer Center, Physical Education, and Parking lot 6.

EXAMPLE: B: *Where's the Music Building?*
      A: *It's across from the Conference Center.*

♦ Write the information on the map.

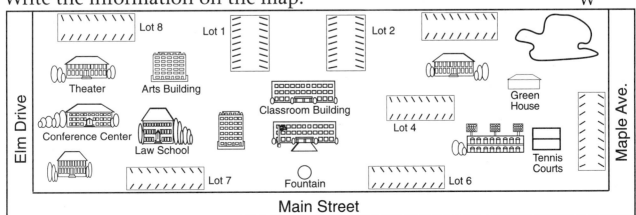

DIALOGUE

HANDOUT 26-C

Carol Washington comes to Crossroads Café to talk to Mr. Brashov. What do they talk about?

Work with a partner.
Read the dialogue cards below.
Put the conversation in order while you watch the video.
Share with another pair. Is the order of the cards the same?

✂ --

ALL: Hi. How are you doing, Carol?

CAROL: But I'd like to talk to you, Victor, if you've got a minute.

MR. BRASHOV: Why don't we step into my office?

MARIE: Thanks for helping out, Katherine.

MR. BRASHOV: I know exactly what you mean.

CAROL: Victor, there's something I'd like you to have.

MR. BRASHOV: Carol . . . I can't take these.

CAROL: I couldn't possibly take this trip.

CAROL: This would make him very happy.

CAROL: Don't wait for the perfect time to do anything.

INTERVIEW

HANDOUT 26-D

Think about Edgar Villarmarin's life in the United States. Is your life similar or different?

- Interview a partner about his or her life in the United States.
- Ask the questions below.
- Add two more questions.
- Write the answers in the chart.
- Share the interview with another pair or the class.

NAME:	INTERVIEWER:
1. When did you come to the United States?	
2. How old were you?	
3. What did you do first (go to school, get a job)?	
4. Did you have any goals? What were they?	
5. Have you achieved any of your goals? Which ones?	
6. Do you have any new goals? What are they?	
7. How will you achieve your new goals?	
8. What advice do you have for newcomers to the United States?	
9.	
10.	

It's early afternoon at Crossroads Café, and Mr. Brashov is thinking about Jess. Mr. Brashov misses Jess a lot.

Jihan comes in the café to see Jamal. Jihan tells Jamal, "I have found a company to ship our things to Egypt." Jamal surprises Jihan when he says, "I don't think we should move back to Egypt." They discuss their decision to return to Egypt, and finally, Jihan agrees with Jamal. They will stay in the United States.

Carol Washington is at home with her son, Daryl. Someone knocks at the door. It's Mr. Brashov. He is holding a shopping bag. Mr. Brashov has something for Carol. It's a chess board—the one he and Jess used to play chess.

Carol shows Mr. Brashov an envelope with tickets for a cruise to the Greek Islands. She wanted to surprise Jess on their anniversary, but now Jess is gone. When Mr. Brashov leaves, Carol cries.

Katherine makes a surprise visit to the café. She shows Rosa a catalogue from City College. Henry stops working to talk to Katherine, too. But Marie tells him to get back to work.

A few minutes later, Henry has an accident. His hand is bleeding. While Marie helps Henry, Katherine waits on the customers. Henry tells Marie, "You should have been a nurse." Marie tells Henry, "I am."

Marie was a nurse in Haiti. She has to go back to school before she can be a nurse in the United States. Henry doesn't like to talk about going to school. He wants to be a rock star, not a student. Marie advises Henry to go to college.

Carol Washington comes in the café to talk to Mr. Brashov. This time Carol has something for Mr. Brashov. She gives him the tickets for the cruise to the Greek Islands. At first, Mr. Brashov doesn't want to accept the tickets. But finally he takes them—for Jess.

A few days later, Mr. Brashov walks around the café with a businessman, Mr. Clayborne. When Mr. Clayborne leaves, Mr. Brashov surprises everyone. He tells them "Mr. Clayborne is the new owner of Crossroads Café. I am 65-years old, and I want to enjoy my life."

It's a week later. The café is closed, but Mr. Brashov and Mr. Clayborne are talking. Jamal comes in with a box and news for Mr. Brashov. He and Jihan changed their minds again. This time they have definitely decided to return to Egypt. Mr. Clayborne also has news for Mr. Brashov. He will bring his own employees to Crossroads Café.

Jamal stops to talk to Henry, Rosa, and Marie. Henry has some news, too. He is going to go to college. Jamal congratulates Henry.

A few minutes later, Mr. Brashov says good-bye to Mr. Clayborne. Now it is Mr. Brashov's turn to give Rosa some news. Mr. Clayborne is not going to be the owner of Crossroads Café. Mr. Brashov has decided to keep the café and hire a manager. The new manager is Rosa Rivera!

GLOSSARY

behavior study

Behavior study is a video technique. Learners view a story clip and watch characters for verbal and nonverbal cues that indicate how they feel.

Use *behavior study* when you want learners to discuss the ways characters interact or when you want to predict future character behavior.

Here is an example of *behavior study.*

- Show a story clip of Rosa looking at an apartment for rent.
- Ask learners, "How can you tell the apartment manager does not want to rent an apartment to Rosa?"

best idea only

Best idea only is a cooperative learning structure. Each pair or group shares its best idea with the class.

Use it to debrief pair or group work.

Here is an example of *best idea only.*

- Katherine's son is very angry at her. He has a bad attitude at home and in school.
- Pairs or groups discuss ways Katherine can help her son.
- Each pair or group shares its best idea with the class.

brainstorming

Brainstorming is used to discover what learners know about a topic or to generate as many ideas as possible about a topic. It's often used as a prereading, prelistening, or prewriting activity. Learners can then organize or use the information in a variety of follow-up activities.

Brainstorming can be done individually, in pairs, in small groups, or as a whole class activity. When *brainstorming,* encourage learners to accept all ideas without discussion of their merit. Stress that all ideas are valid and no judgments should be made.

Here is an example of *brainstorming.*

- Ask learners, "What does Mr. Brashov do at work?"
- Write all of the responses on the board.

clustering

Clustering organizes ideas into categories. *Clustering* adds a visual dimension to learning and is often accompanied by brainstorming.

A circle is drawn around a topic. As key words or ideas are mentioned, lines are drawn from the circle to the new word or idea. Responses can then be grouped together using symbols, underlining, or circling.

Here is an example of *clustering*.

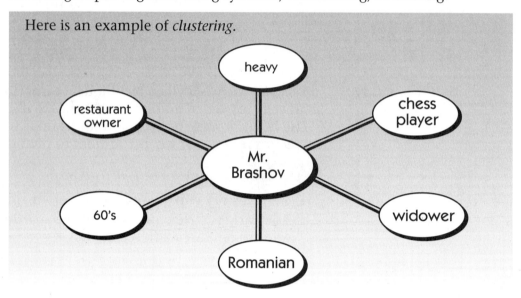

cooperative learning structures

Cooperative learning structures are used to manage and organize learning. These structures stress participation, teamwork, leadership, interaction, accountability, and content mastery.

The Teacher's Resource Book uses these cooperative learning structures: best idea only, corners, roundrobin, roundtable, jigsaw, think-pair-share, line up, and 3-step interview.

For more information about cooperative learning see *Cooperative Learning Resources for Teachers* by Spencer Kagan. Resources for Teachers, Inc., Kagan Cooperative Learning: San Juan Capistrano, CA, 1994.

corners

Corners is a cooperative learning structure that is used for large group discussions.

Learners go to classroom corners that correspond to their opinions, ideas, likes, dislikes, etc. They share the reasons for their choices with others in the same corner. Then someone from each corner shares with the rest of the class.

Here is an example of a *corners* activity.

♦ Go to the corner of the room with the name of the person you are most like: Jamal, Rosa, Henry, or Katherine.
♦ Discuss why you are like this person, make a list, and report to the rest of the class.

A variation is to use three corners or two sides of the room.

culture comparison

Culture comparison is a video technique used for making cross-cultural comparisons.

Learners view a story clip. Then they discuss or write about whether or not what they saw would be the same in their native countries.

> Here is an example of *culture comparison*.
>
> Mr. Brashov is in the hospital. Jamal brings him some food to eat, but the nurse says Mr. Brashov cannot have it. Learners discuss this question:
>
> "What can you bring to a hospital patient in your country?"

freeze frame

Freeze frame is a video technique in which a scene is frozen on the screen so that learners can discuss what they see. You need a pause button on your VCR to use it.

> Here is an example of *freeze frame*.
>
> ♦ A **Culture Clip** shows an apartment that needs a lot of repair.
> ♦ Press the pause button.
> ♦ Ask learners to describe everything they see.

information gap

An *information gap* is an activity that requires a learner to work with a partner to complete a map, table, chart, menu, etc., that has missing information. Partners take turns asking and answering questions and filling in the missing information.

Information gaps create situations that require real communication because one partner has information the other needs. Information gaps also encourage the use of clarification skills and other strategies to negotiate meaning.

> Here is an example of an *information gap* activity.
>
> ♦ Partner A has a bus schedule from which a number of departure times have been deleted.
> ♦ Partner B's schedule has the departure times.
> ♦ Partner B's schedule is missing a number of destinations (stops).
> ♦ Partner A's schedule has the destinations.
> ♦ Partners A and B take turns asking each other questions in order to complete their schedules. As they do so, they are practicing all four skill areas in English.

jigsaw

Jigsaw is a cooperative learning structure that is often used as a reading activity. It works on the same principles as jigsaw puzzles.

Learners are given pieces of a puzzle, or in this case parts of a reading passage, that they must put together. Each learner is responsible for reading and understanding one part and sharing it with the rest of the group. When all of the parts are put together, everyone has the information.

Here is how *jigsaw* works:

♦ Divide class into groups of 3–6 learners. These groups are called **home teams**.

♦ Learners in each group are given numbers that correspond to a number of a reading passage.

♦ If the group has 4–6 people, several people will have the same number.

♦ The teacher or tutor distributes the readings or posts them on the walls. Learners with number one receive reading number one. Everyone with number one works together. They are **expert team one**.

♦ Learners leave their **home teams** and go to their new or **expert teams** where they read and answer questions, helping each other as necessary.

♦ When learners have completed their **expert team** assignment, they return to their **home team** and share information.

♦ Learners from each **expert team** share what they learned with their **home team**.

The drawing below shows how the teams work.

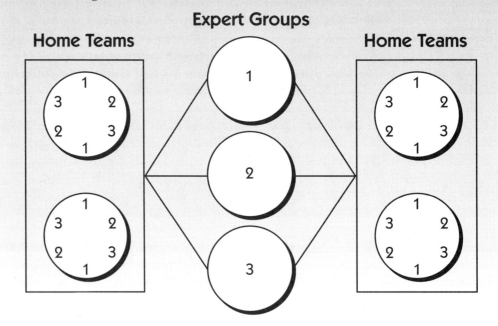

Home Teams · Expert Groups · Home Teams

prediction

Prediction is a video technique. Learners view a story clip and make guesses about what will happen next. After viewing the next clip, they confirm or reject their guesses.

Prediction is used to access learners' prior knowledge, build vocabulary, and enhance their involvement in the video.

Here is an example of *prediction.*

- In Episode 3, Miguel comes to visit Rosa. He wants to get married and return with Rosa to Mexico.
- Replay the two scenes of Rosa and Miguel in her apartment. Ask learners if they think Rosa will return to Mexico.
- Then replay the scene in which Rosa reveals her decision.

role-play

Role-play is an activity that requires learners to pretend to be a different person.

Role-play encourages learners to apply classroom language to real-life situations.

Here is an example of *role-play.*

- One learner is an employer and the other is a job applicant.
- The learners "act out" a job interview.

A variation is to have learners work in groups of three; the third person observes the other two role-play and provides feedback to them.

roundtable and roundrobin

Roundtable and *Roundrobin* are cooperative learning techniques. In roundtable learners write their responses. In roundrobin learners give the responses orally. Roundrobin is sometimes called a share-a-round. It is used when participation rather than a product is the goal or when students have difficulty writing.

Both are used for brainstorming or giving information.

Here is an example of *roundtable.*

- The teacher gives the learners a task, such as to list items of food or to create questions they would ask in a job interview.
- The teacher gives a piece of paper to each group.
- Learner #1 writes a response and then passes the paper to Learner #2.
- Each learner writes a response on the paper.
- The paper literally goes round the table.

Here is an example of *roundrobin.*

- The teacher gives the learners a task, such as to list items of food or to create questions they would ask in a job interview.
- Members of each group take turns within their group, sharing their responses orally.

sides	*Sides* is a variation of **corners**. Please see the description of corners.

silent viewing

Silent viewing is a video technique. A story clip is shown without sound. Learners watch the clip and tell what the characters are doing or what they think they are saying. Then they watch the clip again to find out if they are right.

Silent viewing is a variation of behavior study; learners pay attention to nonverbal behavior to answer questions about the dialogue or actions of the characters.

Here is an example of *silent viewing*.

- It's early in the morning. Mr. Brashov is getting ready to unlock the door to Crossroads Café. To his surprise, the door is already unlocked.
- The scene continues as Mr. Brashov discovers the café has been vandalized.
- Learners retell what happened and then decide what Mr. Brashov said.

sound only

Sound only is a video technique that uses only the audio portion of a video.

Learners listen to a story clip so they can focus on language only. Then they watch the clip again with sound and picture.

Here is an example of *sound only*.

- Teacher describes scene: *Carol and Jess Washington's house has been burglarized. They are meeting with a home security salesperson.*
- Teacher provides focus for listening: *Listen to the conversation and make a list of all of the safety ideas mentioned.*
- Teacher elicits ideas and guides confirmation.
- Students listen and watch again to check their lists.

stand up and share

Stand up and share is a cooperative learning structure used after small group or pair discussions to provide feedback to the whole class.

Here is an example of *stand up and share*.

- The entire class stands up.
- The teacher asks a volunteer to share with the class.
- Learners with the same idea or answer sit down.
- The activity ends when all learners have sat down.

teams share

Teams share is a cooperative learning structure used to provide feedback. One member of a group (team) moves to another group to share information about what its home team has been doing or discussing.

> Here is an example of *teams share.*
> - Give learners in each group a number.
> - After learners have completed their group assignment, say, "Number one in each group move to another group and share what your group discussed."

telling the story

Telling the story is a video technique. Learners take turns retelling the story or a story clip in their own words. It can be used for summarizing the entire video or selected story clips.

A variation is for learners to purposely change some key facts in their retelling and have other learners "catch" the mistakes.

thinking and feeling

Thinking and feeling is a video technique that focuses learners' attention on what characters are thinking and/or feeling during a story clip. If you want learners to concentrate on nonverbal language, you can combine this technique with *silent viewing*.

> Here is an example of *thinking and feeling.*
> - Miguel asks Rosa to marry him, but she turns him down.
> - Ask learners to guess what Miguel and Rosa are thinking, not saying, while they are talking.
> - Ask learners to describe how Rosa and Miguel feel.
> - Have volunteers role-play situations where Miguel and Rosa tell others about what happened.

A variation of this is *thinking and feeling* with *silent viewing.* Have learners watch a story clip without the sound and write or role-play the dialogue.

think-pair-share

Think-pair-share is a cooperative learning technique used to promote discussion and provide feedback. It has three steps.

- Learners think of questions or issues.
- Learners are given time to think of responses.
- Learners share their responses with a partner.

> Here is an example of *think-pair-share*.
> - Ask learners to think about what they did and how they felt on their first day in the United States.
> - Have learners write five things they did and felt.
> - Have learners share their lists with a partner by asking and answering questions. Learners do not show their lists to each other because doing so would eliminate the need to talk.

3-step interview

3-step interview is a cooperative learning technique used to promote discussion and develop listening skills.

There are three steps to follow when doing *three-step interviews*.

- Divide class into groups of four learners. Tell them the discussion topic.
- Give members of each group a number from 1–4.
- Learner 1 interviews learner 2 while learner 3 interviews learner 4. (Step One)
- Learner 2 interviews learner 1 while learner 4 interviews learner 3. (Step Two)
- Learner 1 shares what he or she has learned from learner 2 and so on until each learner has shared with the group. (Step Three)

You can further debrief the groups by using *best idea only*, or *stand up and share*, or *teams share*.

Total Physical Response (TPR)

TPR is a method for teaching and learning languages based on giving and following commands. A basic premise is that associating language with physical activity accelerates language learning.

TPR is used to teach learners at all proficiency levels. Beginning-level learners respond to and give simple commands such as "stand up" or "sit down"; intermediate-level learners take turns following and giving instructions for making something (like popcorn); and advanced-level learners give more complicated, multi-step directions such as returning an item to a store.

James Asher, a psychologist, is the creator of *TPR*. See *Techniques and Principles in Language Teaching* by Diane Larsen-Freeman. Oxford University Press, 1986, for more information.

Venn diagrams

Venn diagrams are intersecting circles. These graphic organizers, or ways to visually depict ideas, are often used in discussion or writing to show differences and commonalities.

- Learners draw two intersecting circles.
- Each circle represents one of the two things being compared.
- Learners write differences in the portion of the circles that don't intersect.
- Learners write similarities in the space where the circles intersect.

Here is an example of a *Venn diagram* that compares Rosa and Katherine.

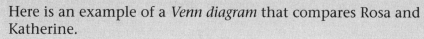

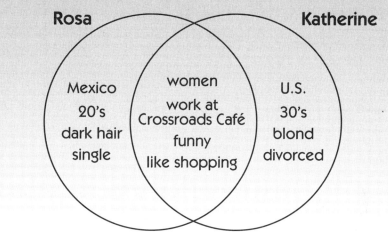

watchers and listeners

Watchers and listeners is a video technique used to discuss a story clip. It develops conversation, listening, and clarification skills.

Partner A is a watcher of the video and Partner B is a listener.

Here is an example of *watchers and listeners*.

- Learners are divided into pairs.
- One person in each pair is **A**, and the other is **B**.
- **A** watches a story clip from the video. **B** has his or her back to the TV/VCR and listens to the story clip.
- After the clip has been shown, **A** and **B** have a set of questions to answer. **A** (the watcher) answers using information he or she has seen. **B** (the listener) answers using information he or she has heard.

WAYS TO LEARN CHECKLIST

	STRATEGY	INITIAL ASSESSMENT			RECORD OF ACTIVITY		FUTURE GOAL
		Circle one letter: P = poor G = good E = excellent			Date	Comments	
14	Make a List	P	G	E			
15	Make Inferences	P	G	E			
16	Try and Try Again	P	G	E			
17	Read for Meaning	P	G	E			
18	Be Open to Learning	P	G	E			
19	Take a Risk	P	G	E			

	STRATEGY	INITIAL ASSESSMENT			RECORD OF ACTIVITY		FUTURE GOAL
		Circle one letter: P = poor G = good E = excellent			Date	Comments	
20	Take Notes	P	G	E			
21	Teach Others	P	G	E			
22	Practice Often	P	G	E			
23	Know Your Learning Style	P	G	E			
24	Look for Humor	P	G	E			
25	Compliment Yourself	P	G	E			
26	Evaluate Your Learning	P	G	E			